# LITERATURE GUIDE

## LITERATURE GUIDE

## Key Stage 3

# Henry V

First published 2003
exclusively for WHSmith by
Hodder & Stoughton Educational
338 Euston Road
London
NW1 3BH

ISBN 0 340 87284 5

Copyright © 2003 Shaun McCarthy
Introduction ('How to study') copyright © 2003 Tony Buzan

All rights reserved. No part of this publication may be reproduced or transmitted in any form or by any means, electronic or mechanical, including photocopying, recording or any information storage and retrieval system, without permission in writing from the publisher or under licence from the Copyright Licensing Agency Limited. Further details of such licences (for reprographic reproduction) may be obtained from the Copyright Licensing Agency Limited, of 90 Tottenham Court Road, London W1P 9HE

Illustrations: Karen Donnelly and David Ashby
Mind Maps ®: Anne Jones

Typeset by Transet Limited, Leamington Spa, England.
Printed in Great Britain for Hodder & Stoughton Educational, a division of Hodder Headline Plc, 338 Euston Road, London NW1 3BH by Cox & Wyman Ltd., Reading, Berkshire.

# Contents

| | |
|---|---|
| **H**ow to study | vii |
| **H**ow to use this guide | xi |
| **T**he story of *Henry V* | 1 |
| **C**haracters | 7 |
| *The English* | |
| ●Henry V, King of England | 7 |
| ●The loyal nobles | 8 |
| ●The conspirators | 8 |
| ●The Army | 9 |
| ●The Church | 9 |
| ●Henry's former 'common' friends | 9 |
| *The French* | |
| ●The Royal Family | 11 |
| ●French nobles | 11 |
| ●Other French characters | 12 |
| **C**ommentary | 14 |
| **M**odel answer | 70 |
| **H**ints on the Shakespeare exam | 75 |
| **G**lossary | 79 |
| **I**ndex | 81 |

# HOW TO STUDY

## Your magnificent 'Memory Muscle'

Your memory is like a muscle. If you don't use it, it will grow weaker and weaker, but if you do keep it exercised, it will grow stronger and stronger. Here are four tips for improving your memory:

1 **Work for between 20 and 40 minutes at a time, and then take a break.** This allows your Memory Muscle to rest and lets the information sink in.
2 **Go back over your work.** Wait for a little while after you have been learning something, and then look back at it later; you'll catch your brain at the top of the memory wave and remember even more.
3 **Make connections.** Your Memory Muscle becomes stronger when it can link things together. Join the separate facts together in some way to make a picture, for example on a Mind Map, and they'll come back to you all together, in a flash!
4 **Think big.** Your Memory Muscle gets stronger if what it is trying to remember is special in some way, so 'think big' and make what you are learning brightly coloured, funny, peculiar, special.

## Your new magic learning formula – the Mind Map®

The Mind Map is a very special map. It helps you to find your way around a subject easily and quickly because it mirrors the way your brain works. Use it for organizing your work both at school and at home, for taking notes and planning your homework.

### THE MIND MAPS IN THIS BOOK

Look at the Mind Map on p. 13. In the centre is a picture which summarizes the theme of the topic. Coming out from this there are several branches, each one covering an important part of the topic.

### HOW TO READ A MIND MAP

1 Begin in the centre, the focus of your topic.
2 The words/images attached to the centre are like chapter headings: read them next.
3 Always read out from the centre, in every direction (even on the left-hand side, where you will have to read from right to left, instead of the usual left to right).

### HOW TO DRAW A MIND MAP

1 Start in the middle of the page with the page turned sideways. This gives your brain the maximum width for its thoughts.
2 Always start by drawing a small picture or symbol. Why? Because a picture is worth a thousand words to your brain. And try to use at least three colours, as colour helps your memory even more.
3 Write or draw your ideas on coloured branching lines connected to your central image. These key symbols and words are the headings for your topic.
4 Then add facts, further items and ideas by drawing more, smaller, branches on to the main branches, just like a tree.
5 Always print your word clearly on its line. Use only one word per line.
6 To link ideas and thoughts on different branches, use arrows, colours, underlining and boxes.

You see how easy it is! You have summarized an entire topic on just one page, and this is now firmly logged in your brain, for you to get at whenever you want! If you look at this Mind Map five times over the next five months, the information it contains will be in your brain for many, many years to come.

## Make life easy for your brain

When you start on a new book or topic there are several things you can do to help get your brain 'on line' faster:

1 Quickly scan through the whole book or topic.
2 Think of what you already know about the subject.
3 Ask 'who?', 'what?', 'why?', 'where?', 'when?' and 'how?' questions about your topic.

4 Have another quick scan through.
5 Build up a Mind Map.
6 Mark up any difficult bits and move on.
7 Have a final scan.

And finally, have fun while you learn.

# HOW TO USE THIS GUIDE

This guide will help you whether you are reading the whole play or just an extract of one or two scenes – referred to in this guide as 'Hot scenes'. It will help you to understand and enjoy the play, and to revise.

## WHICH BITS SHOULD I READ?

If possible, read the whole play and the whole guide! However, lots of students just read the extract. This is all right, but you should at least know the full story of the play. You will then be able to see how the extract fits in. For the story, read the guide section 'The story of *Henry V*'.

You will also understand the extract better if you know something about all the characters in the play. So read the 'Characters' section, focusing on characters in the extract.

Definitely read what the 'Commentary' has to say about the extract you are studying. The 'Key ideas' and 'Style' sections take you deeper into the scene. The 'Word from Will' boxes give useful background.

The 'Model answer' shows you what a really good exam answer is like. Don't try to copy it, but read the notes on what's good about it.

The Glossary explains special words or phrases used in the guide (typed in **bold**).

## QUESTIONS

In the 'Commentary' there are questions marked with a star ✪. Think about these to develop your own ideas. They do not normally have a single right answer.

At the end of each 'Hot scene' there is a 'Hotspot' with questions and activities. These will help you to develop your ideas and remember what you have learned. You could take a

xi

break *before* this, but you should certainly take one *after* the Hotspot before re-reading the scene or doing other work.

*Henry V* is one of Shakespeare's ten history plays, which means that it is based on real events and people. Remember that Shakespeare had to make it into a piece of popular drama, so used his imagination to fill in the gaps from the history books he read. Most of the history available then was written from the royal family's point of view. Shakespeare tends to give the 'official' side of the story – but he does not always make royalty look perfect.

If you watch the video of the play, starring Kenneth Branagh, it will help you to understand the play even better – remember, Shakespeare wrote plays to be watched. He wanted his audience to enjoy themselves – otherwise he wouldn't have made any money!

# THE STORY OF *HENRY V*

## *WILD CHILD TO WISE MAN*

Henry has become king of England. During his father's reign, Henry, often nicknamed 'Hal' or 'Harry', was rather a wild young prince, but in this play we see him growing up fast and becoming a loved and respected king.

## *WHEELING AND DEALING*

At the beginning of the play, Henry has surprised everyone with his cleverness and piety (devotion to God). However, Archbishop Canterbury and Bishop Ely are worried that a proposed new law will take away a lot of the Church's wealth. In the meantime, the King is thinking about invading France because he believes that he has a claim to the throne. Canterbury thinks that if the Church promises money to help with the French war then Henry will stop the law being passed. So Canterbury backs the King and the lords also urge him to invade France.

## *GAME, SET AND MATCH*

After receiving a scornful gift of tennis balls from the Dauphin (the heir to the French throne), Henry threatens war.

## *BETRAYAL*

Henry brings together an army and a fleet at Southampton. While there, he uncovers a plot – three of his followers have been bribed by the French to assassinate him. They are arrested and executed for treason.

# HENRY V

## *UNSUITABLE FRIENDS*

Another sign that Henry is taking his kingship seriously is that he has got rid of some old friends. Before this play begins Henry was close to Sir John Falstaff and his followers, Pistol, Nym, Bardolph and the Boy. Young Henry used to drink with them all at Mistress Quickly's inn. Falstaff was a great friend but a drunken and irresponsible old knight and his followers were no better. Henry turns his back on Falstaff once he becomes the King because the friendship would be bad for his reputation. The Hostess (Mistress Quickly) believes that Falstaff's heart was broken by the King's rejection, and caused his illness.

## *WIN OR LOSE?*

When Henry lands in France with his army he sends ambassadors to Charles VI, the French king, to demand the crown. Charles offers his daughter in marriage and also some dukedoms in France, but Henry rejects the offer. Instead, he captures the town of Harfleur. He leaves some of his army to guard it and takes the rest towards Calais. However, his army is small and many of the soldiers are sick, so the chances of him winning a battle against the French are poor.

## *GOTCHA!*

The French gather a large army and stop Henry's troops near Agincourt, where a huge and bloody battle takes place. Despite having a much bigger army than the English, the French are defeated and Henry returns to England in triumph.

## *WINNER TAKES ALL*

Finally, a meeting takes place between Henry and Charles and a peace treaty is signed. From this, it is agreed that Henry will marry Katherine, the French princess, and he will also be recognized as heir to the French throne. Henry woos Katherine and the play ends with friendship and prayers that England and France will be at peace.

# THE STORY OF *HENRY V*

# Test *yourself*

Circle the right answers in the account of the story below. Then check your answers by referring back.

## WILD CHILD TO WISE MAN

Henry has become king of England. During his father's reign, Henry, often nicknamed 'Hal' or 'Harry', was rather a wild young prince, but in this play we see him growing up fast and becoming a (**despised / weak / loved and respected**) king.

## WHEELING AND DEALING

At the beginning of the play, Henry has surprised everyone with his cleverness and piety (devotion to God). However, Archbishop Canterbury and Bishop Ely are worried that a new law will take away a lot of the Church's wealth. In the meantime, the King is thinking about invading France because he believes that he has (**fallen in love with Katherine / to protect England / a claim to the throne of France**). Canterbury thinks that if the Church promises money to help with the French war then Henry will (**favour the Church / stop the law being passed / forget about war**). So Canterbury backs the King and the lords also urge him to invade France.

## GAME, SET AND MATCH

After a (**scornful / humorous / confusing**) message from the Dauphin (**the French King / an ambassador / the heir to the French throne**), Henry threatens war.

## BETRAYAL

Henry brings together an army and a fleet at Southampton. While there, he uncovers a plot – three of his followers have been bribed by the French to assassinate him. They are arrested and (**executed / pardoned / sent to France**) for treason.

3

# HENRY V

# The story of Henry V

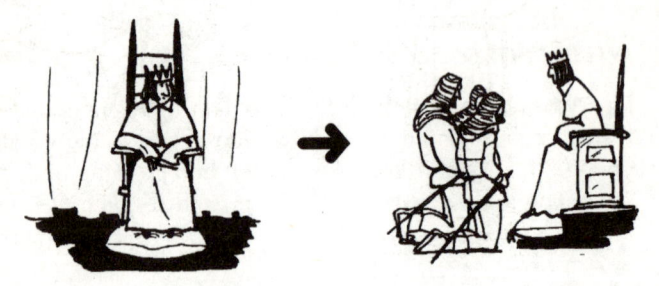

## MAIN PLOT

**The King's Palace** – Churchmen, salic law, tennis balls and plans for war.

**Southampton** – the conspirators uncovered.

**Rouen** – Learning English, and defeating them!

**Agincourt** – the dark night before ... And victory.

## SUBPLOT

**The Boar's Head** – Pistol (skinny rogue) and company hear Falstaff is sick.

**The Boar's Head** – Falstaff's dead, off to France.

# THE STORY OF *HENRY V*

**Rouen** – Exeter warns the French.

**Harfleur** – *Once more into the breach ...* And victory.

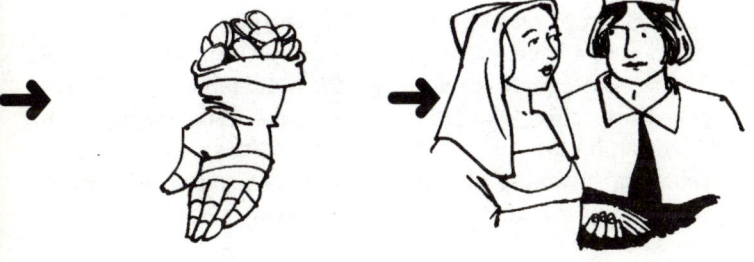

**Agincourt** – A glove full of crowns.

**Troyes** – Henry has Katherine's hand in marriage.

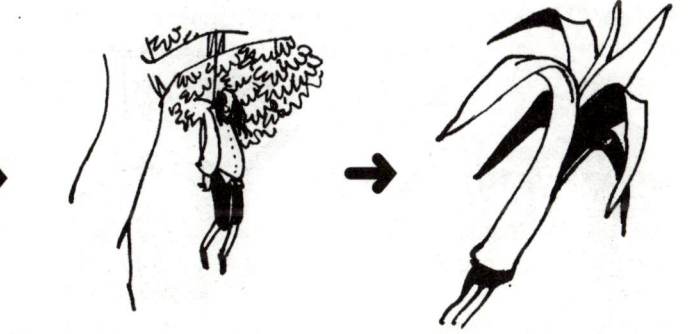

**France** – Bardolph is hanged.

**France** – Pistol forced to eat a leek.

# HENRY V

## *UNSUITABLE FRIENDS*

Another sign that Henry is taking his kingship seriously is that he has got rid of some old friends. Before this play begins Henry was close to Sir John Falstaff and his followers, Pistol, Nym, Bardolph and the Boy. Young Henry used to drink with them all at Mistress Quickly's inn. Falstaff was a great friend but a drunken and irresponsible old knight and his followers were no better. Henry turns his back on Falstaff once he becomes the King because the friendship would be bad for his reputation. The Hostess (Mistress Quickly) believes that Falstaff's heart was broken by the King's rejection, and caused his (**absence / anger / illness**).

## *WIN OR LOSE?*

When Henry lands in France with his army he sends ambassadors to Charles VI, the French king, to demand the crown. Charles offers his daughter in marriage and also some dukedoms in France, but Henry (**considers / accepts / rejects**) the offer. Instead, he captures the town of Harfleur. He leaves some of his army to guard it and takes the rest towards Calais. However, his army is small and many of the soldiers are (**rebelling / wanting to make peace / sick**), so the chances of him winning a battle against the French are poor.

## *GOTCHA!*

The French gather a large army and stop Henry's troops near (**Calais / Harfleur / Agincourt**), where a huge and bloody battle takes place. Despite having a much bigger army than the English, the French are defeated and Henry returns to England in triumph.

## *WINNER TAKES ALL*

Finally, a meeting takes place between Henry and Charles and a peace treaty is signed. From this, it is agreed that Henry will marry Katherine, the French princess, and (**Katherine / the Dauphin / Henry**) will also be recognized as heir to the French throne. Henry woos Katherine and the play ends with friendship and prayers that England and France will be at peace.

# CHARACTERS

*Henry V* is about action more than characters. The only person whose inner thoughts we learn about in any detail is Henry. It also has a very large cast. In stage productions parts are usually 'doubled' (one actor takes two or more smaller parts).

## The English

### Henry V, King of England

It is important to know that this is the third play in which Henry has appeared. In *Henry IV, Parts 1 and 2*, he is a wild and feckless young man, best friend of drunken Sir John Falstaff. When he becomes king at the end of *Henry IV, Part 2*, Henry immediately drops his old friends. (This is said to be the cause of Falstaff's illness and death, reported in Act 2, scene 1 of *Henry V.*)

This wild past is the reason Canterbury and Ely describe Henry's transformation into a *king full of grace, and fair regard* at such length in the play's opening scene. Henry has changed from a youth whose hours were *filled up with riots, banquets, sports* to a wise king who turned *to any cause of policy,/ The Gordian knot of it he will unloose.* (He can unravel seemingly impossible political problems.)

Henry has become a clever and well-liked king. He is generous to those who are loyal to him. He fills Williams' glove with crowns after the soldier has apologized for arguing with Henry while the king was disguised. He offers any man who doesn't want to fight at Agincourt the chance to leave, and money for their journey.

However, Henry is also ruthless. He doesn't even think of granting Scroop, one of the conspirators and his oldest friend, a reprieve from execution. His threats to the governor of Harfleur to let the English army rape, pillage and burn the town are graphic and lengthy. But many in Shakespeare's day would have seen ruthlessness as a strength in a king, so this cruel side to Henry's character may have seemed less cruel then.

In the scenes before the battle of Agincourt, Henry shows himself able to be a 'man of the people'. He does not reveal any anger when soldiers speak badly of the King. Shakespeare wants to show Henry as a king who has a 'common touch'. Maybe he learnt this from his old drinking friends.

In the play's final scene, when Henry is alone with Katherine, we see another side of him: Henry the lover. It is hard to say much about this. The play is nearly over and he may be trying to impress a woman who does not want to marry him. But he does speak plainly and familiarly to her, calling her *Kate*. In some ways he is doing what he did with the soldiers on the eve of Agincourt, trying to come down from the lofty role of King to the level of an ordinary man. He has described the heavy burdens of kingship (in Act 4, scene1) so he may enjoy being more 'ordinary' when he gets the chance.

## The loyal nobles

- ◆ Gloucester and Bedford (Henry's brothers)
- ◆ Exeter (Henry's Uncle)
- ◆ Westmorland and York (Henry's cousins)
- ◆ Warwick (a lord, but a very minor character)
- ◆ Salisbury (a professional soldier)
- ◆ Sir Thomas Erpingham (a loyal, dignified old knight)

The nobles are all figures in the story rather than fully developed human beings. There are too many of them for us to learn about their private thoughts and feelings. In fact we learn more about the 'common' characters.

## The conspirators

- ◆ Lord Scroop (formerly a close personal friend of Henry V)
- ◆ Earl of Cambridge (flattering hypocrite)
- ◆ Lord Gray (agrees with his co-conspirators)

The conspirators are men that the King should be able to trust. They all have titles. They are part of the power structure of the country that exists to support the King. Furthermore, Scroop was Henry's friend. We never really know what has persuaded them to turn against 'king and country'.

## The Army

- ◆ Llewellyn, a Welsh Captain (called 'Fluellen' in some editions)
- ◆ Gower, an English Captain
- ◆ MacMorris, an Irish Captain
- ◆ Jamy, a Scottish Captain
- ◆ Williams and Bates, English soldiers

The army captains are stereotypes, largely in the story for comic relief, and to represent Henry's entire kingdom. We know relatively little about them as people. Llewellyn is fiercely patriotic, forcing Pistol to eat a raw leek for mocking this emblem of Welsh nationality. He is long-winded, but he is a good, generous man. Gower is his calmer, unimaginative friend. MacMorris is supposed to be 'typically' Irish in his hot-tempered oversensitivity to any hint that Ireland might be criticized.

Williams and Bates are good ordinary men, down-to-earth, loyal and brave. However, Williams refuses to believe that the King would not allow himself to be ransomed to save his life. This leads him to quarrel with Henry – unknowingly, since Henry is in disguise.

## The Church

- ◆ Archbishop of Canterbury (head of the Church, a rather boring expert on the law)
- ◆ Bishop of Ely (backs up Canterbury's views)

## Henry's former 'common' friends

- ◆ Bardolph (red-nosed rogue who tries to stop Nym and Pistol fighting)

# HENRY V

- ◆ Nym (sulky, unintelligent character who likes to present himself as a mystery)
- ◆ Pistol (swaggerer who loves to speak as if he were a hero in an old-fashioned melodrama)
- ◆ Boy (Falstaff's former page)
- ◆ Hostess (Nell Quickly, married to Pistol)

Henry's former drinking friends are minor figures in the story of the war with France. But they are given more character than the nobles. They are the commoners of the story, and many in Shakespeare's audience would have felt more in touch with them than with the brave but serious nobles. Pistol and the rest of the gang are rogues, but they are not evil. They make the audience laugh. And they all show genuine grief when Falstaff dies.

Pistol is the most cunning. After all the high talk of an honourable war, Pistol just wants to go and rob the French. After being beaten and humiliated by Llewellyn, he immediately has a plan for what he will do when he gets back to London.

Only the Boy seems to have any morals. In his soliloquy in Act 3, scene 3, he makes a good study of his companions and decides that he must look to mending his own ways. He sees himself being encouraged to be a pickpocket, and he knows that to be wrong. And in another soliloquy, in Act 4, scene 4, he decides to distance himself from Pistol, who he realizes is a coward.

Falstaff is an important influence on these characters, although we never see the old knight in this play. He was Henry's friend and companion in *Henry IV*, Parts 1 and 2, the plays that precede this one in Shakespeare's series of History plays. On becoming the King, Henry immediately dropped the drunken and disreputable Falstaff. Pistol and the others think the cruel way Henry did this drove Falstaff into his fatal illness.

CHARACTERS

# The French

## The Royal Family

- King Charles VI (a cautious king)
- Queen Isabel (Charles' queen)
- The Dauphin, their eldest son (proud, boastful playboy)
- Princess Katherine (shy daughter to Charles and Isabel)

## French nobles

- Dukes of Berri, Bourbon, Orleans, Burgundy
- Constable of France

# HENRY V

## Other French characters

- Alice, lady in waiting to princess Katherine
- Governor of Harfleur
- French Ambassador
- Mountjoy, a herald
- Monsieur le Fer

The French are really just 'the enemy'. Some, such as Mountjoy the Herald and Burgundy, might appear more brave or reasonable than the others, but none of the French are fully developed characters. You could describe each of them in a word or two; for example, the Dauphin – proud and boastful, the King – hesitant, cautious.

We learn a bit more about Katherine, whom we briefly see leading a private life (laughing with her *gentlewoman* Alice in Act 3, scene 5). But we get no idea of what she thinks about being betrothed Henry. Is she attracted to this foreign king? Or is she humiliated by being really just a trophy given to the victor? We never know. ✪ What do you imagine Katherine thinks about her coming marriage to Henry?

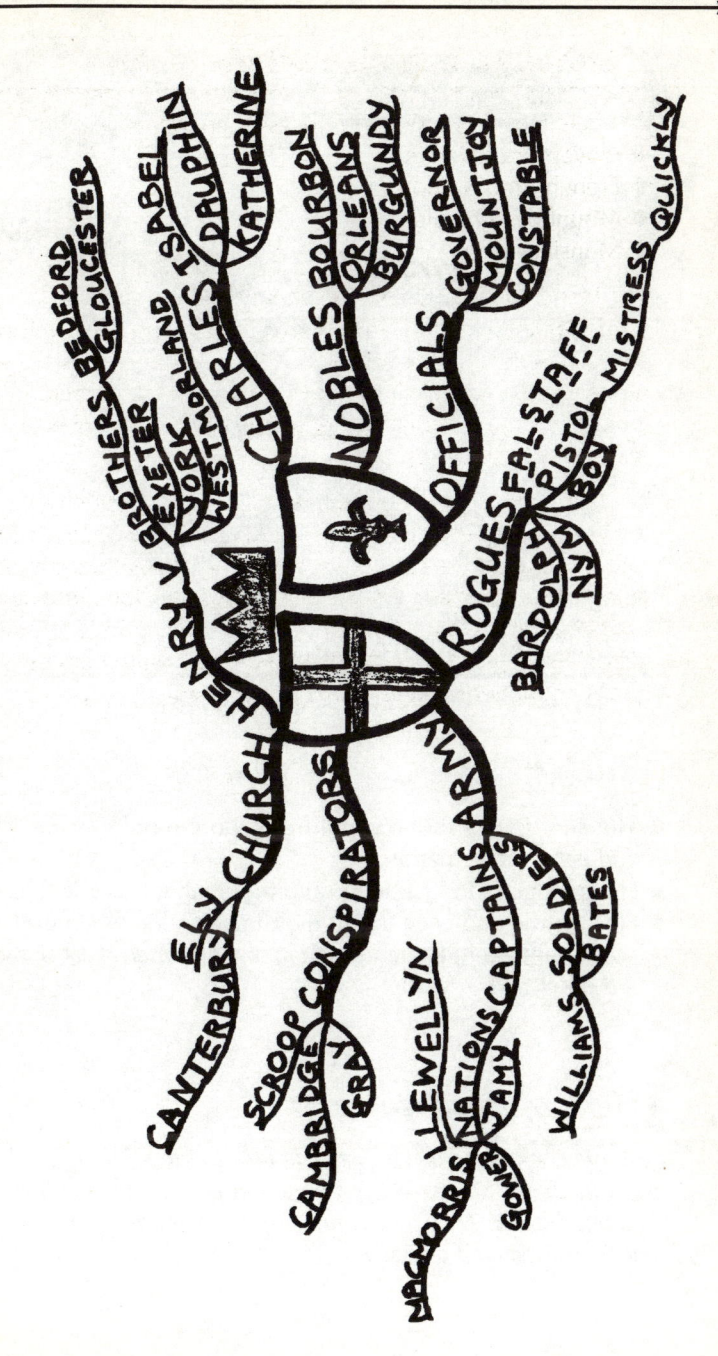

CHARACTERS

- Henry
  - Brothers
    - Bedford
    - Gloucester
  - Exeter
  - York
  - Westmorland
- Charles
  - Isabel
  - Dauphin
  - Katherine
- Nobles
  - Bourbon
  - Orleans
  - Burgundy
- Officials
  - Governor
  - Mountjoy
  - Constable
- Rogues
  - Falstaff
  - Pistol
  - Mistress Quickly
  - Boy
  - Nym
  - Bardolph
- Church
  - Canterbury
  - Ely
- Conspirators
  - Cambridge
  - Scroop
  - Gray
- Army
  - Captains
    - Llewellyn
    - Nations
      - Jamy
      - Gower
      - Macmorris
  - Soldiers
    - Williams
    - Bates

## COMMENTARY

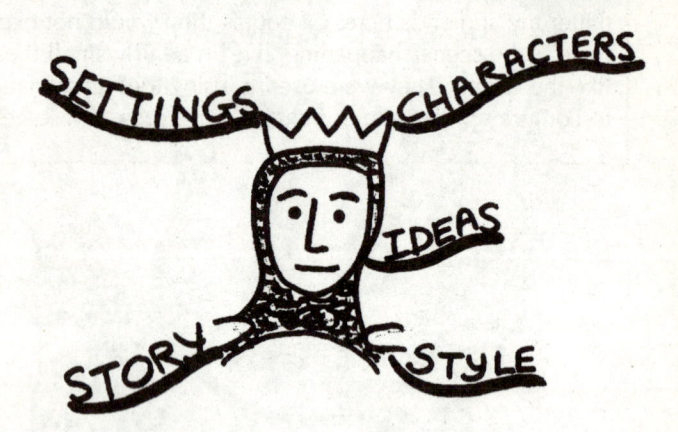

### Act 1, The Prologue

An actor speaks to the audience about the play.

#### SUMMARY

- ◆ The chorus asks for powerful inspiration in order to grab the audience's imagination.
- ◆ He apologizes for the actors and the smallness of the theatre.
- ◆ He asks the audience to use their imagination when the scene shifts from England to France, and when great battles are described.

## Tricks of the theatre

*Can this cockpit hold/ The vasty fields of France?* Imagine watching battle scenes played by a handful of actors in a small wooden theatre! The Chorus refers to the theatre as *this wooden O,* as well as *cockpit.*

# COMMENTARY

### A word from Will

I was setting out to write a popular play, so I was trying to flatter my audience here. Of course they would not expect huge battle scenes happening 'live' in a fairly small theatre like the Globe! They were used to using their imaginations to conjure up vast armies fighting somewhere 'off stage'.

## STYLE

There are lots of clues here about the way Shakespeare wants us to think about Henry. Firstly, he is compared to Mars, the god of war. Then *famine*, *sword* and *fire* are described like fierce dogs that he controls.

### Act 1, scene 1: *Church in crisis*

Two church leaders discuss a new law that will take away money from the Church. They also discuss the King.

**Setting:** London, a room in King Henry's palace. This meeting is secret, so a director might make the scene dark and shadowy.

# HENRY V

**SUMMARY**

- ◆ Canterbury and Ely discuss their worries about a bill (a new law) to tax the Church.
- ◆ They discuss how much Henry has changed.
- ◆ Canterbury has promised the King money to help fight the French if the bill is stopped.

## Tax the Church?

The Church was a very powerful organization at this time, second only to the monarchy. It helped the poor and sick, but there were also greedy Churchmen. The bill would take half the Church's wealth and do two important things with it. Firstly, it would give King Henry money to pay noblemen to support him in times of war and peace. Secondly, it would help the poor and sick. So, the first part would increase the King's power, whereas the second part would give charity to the needy.

## Bad boy to respected king

They move on to discuss the change in Henry's behaviour. Ely says, *The strawberry grows underneath the nettle ... the prince obscured his contemplation* [hid his seriousness]/ *Under the veil of wildness.* (Young Henry used to mix with undesirable people, hiding his virtue – the strawberry – under his wild behaviour – the nettle.) Perhaps he was just hiding behind his bad reputation while learning how to become a good king. There are lots of other powerful descriptions of the changes in him. *Consideration* [prayer] *like an angel came .../ Leaving his body as a paradise.* This makes the King sound holy.

## Help from the King?

The bishops believe that the King is *indifferent* (neutral) about the new bill, so he will think carefully about their offer to help him with a war against France.

# COMMENTARY

## STYLE

Notice that when noble characters like the bishops and the King speak, they use **iambic pentameter** (when unrhymed, also called **blank verse**). This is a form of poetry that was popular in drama in Shakespeare's time. You can recognize it easily because it is centred in the middle of the page and if you count the syllables each line has roughly ten.

### Act 1, scene 2: *War or peace?*

This scene begins with a discussion about Henry's right to the French throne. He has already decided to go to war when the French ambassador arrives with an insulting gift from the Dauphin (heir to the French throne).

**Setting:** The council chamber in Henry's palace, London.

### SUMMARY

- ◆ Henry asks the Churchmen if he has a just claim to the French throne. They say he has.
- ◆ Canterbury promises Church money to help with the war.
- ◆ Henry worries that the Scots will invade England if his army goes to France.
- ◆ There is a long conversation about order in the state.
- ◆ Henry vows to win the war or die.
- ◆ The Dauphin sends a rude message to Henry.

This is a vital meeting. The council chamber is full of noblemen and church leaders. It is the powerhouse of England. The atmosphere is formal and grand, reflecting the King's power. Henry is deciding whether to start a war, so the atmosphere is also tense.

## A *just war?*

Henry asks the Archbishop of Canterbury if it can be proved that he has a reasonable claim to the French throne. He warns the Archbishop to give good advice because war causes death and destruction. He needs to be sure he is justified in taking

# HENRY V

such a big step. Henry must have asked the Archbishop to look into this already, because the Archbishop has amassed a whole list of complex proofs.

## Salic law

Canterbury explains that the French are using Salic law to keep their power. Salic law means that no woman shall be allowed to inherit the throne of Salic lands. However, there are two things that contradict this. Firstly, the Salic territories were part of Germany not France, so the law does not apply in France. Secondly, there have been French kings whose claim to the throne came from a female member of the family – just like Henry. In this way, Canterbury proves that Henry is in the right.

---

**A word from Will**

The Archbishop's 'proof' is really complex. Although it is the spur England needs to go to war, I bet half my audience wouldn't have a clue what the Archbishop was on about! To stop them getting bored, the scene can be played with comedy, with Henry striding about the stage, and the two Churchmen scurrying after him dropping pieces of old paper. Or it can be done very seriously, with the King sitting on his throne listening gravely. Most of my audience believed in 'England, right or wrong' anyway.

---

## Decision time

Henry listens to advice, but he is no fool. Canterbury makes a very long and complicated explanation but the King pushes for a straightforward answer. *May I with right and conscience make this claim?* He is saying, 'Let's get to the point'! Canterbury even quotes from the Bible to prove the King's right to fight France.

COMMENTARY

## Pressure

Henry is reminded of his noble ancestors such as Edward the Black Prince, who fought bravely against the French long ago. Henry is under a lot of pressure, but he doesn't just give in and declare war because the bishops and nobles want it. He is worried about the Scots invading England while he is away. This tells us that he cares for his people. He mentions his great-grandfather's problems with the Scots, showing that he knows his history and means to learn from it. We can see that he has a mind of his own.

## Propaganda

All the men in this scene are powerful and wealthy. It is in their interest to make sure that the society that supports them stays like this. This does not mean that they are bad, but they do believe in the 'system' which keeps them as top dogs. Therefore they will look for arguments to make everyone else obey their rules!

## Harmony

Exeter says that government is like *music*. He believes that there is a natural 'harmony' in the country and that even if the *armed hand* is away fighting in France, the *advised head* will keep things going. The fighters might leave, but the advisers will stay – like the other part of a two-part harmony!

## Obedience and co-operation

Canterbury extends this idea. He uses the **metaphor** (comparison) of the beehive, where each bee knows its place and works for the good of all. He says that the bees organize their lives like us, with a queen and so on. Some people agree with this and say it is a realistic picture of a stable society. Others believe it is just propaganda – ideas to persuade ordinary people to do as they are told. ✪ What do you think?

# HENRY V

## Determination

Henry does not rush into war but once he makes up his mind, we can see his strength of character. *Now we are well resolved.* Look at how he uses the royal 'we' when referring to himself – this indicates his power. He makes a vow that if he cannot persuade France to go along with him he will *break it all to pieces.* This is the first sign of ruthlessness that he will show again.

## Don't shoot the messenger!

The French ambassador arrives with an insulting message from the Dauphin. Henry shows fairness by allowing the ambassador to speak freely. The Dauphin's message mocks Henry's wild youth: *there's naught in France/ That can be with a nimble galliard won.* (There is nothing in France that can be won with a lively dance.) The Dauphin's gift of tennis balls means that Henry should stick to games. Shakespeare uses **dramatic irony** here. The audience knows Henry is a clever and brave king, even if the Dauphin does not. Henry turns the tennis joke back on the Dauphin: *We will … play a set/ Shall strike his father's crown into the hazard.* In other words, he will fight so well that he'll defeat the French!

## Deadly serious

Henry does not only make jokes. He uses the idea of tennis balls to issue a deadly threat to the Dauphin: *this mock of his/ Hath turned his balls to gun-stones* (cannonballs). He warns that the Dauphin's *mock* (joke) will cause the French to curse their prince when they are defeated in war.

### 🔑 KEY IDEAS

An important idea in this scene is **power**. The first example is that Henry wants to be sure that he is fighting a war for good reasons. He does not want to abuse his power. The discussion about the beehive is also about power in a kingdom.

# COMMENTARY

Another key idea that runs through the whole play is **patriotism**. The English are very much the 'good guys'. Even Henry's disreputable old friends (Bardolph, etc.) are comic rather than evil. By contrast the French are vain, proud and, in the end, not as good at war as the English. You can imagine Shakespeare's audience cheering on the English in the battles.

It is important that Henry is seen here to have a just claim to the French throne, given all the deaths that will result from his declaration of war against France.

---

**A word from Will**

People in my day were very patriotic. When I was writing *Henry V* in 1599, Queen Elizabeth was preparing to send a great army to fight the Irish. The Irish had already destroyed one English army. A play like *Henry V*, full of noble deeds and heroism, was just the thing to get ordinary people to support a new war.

---

## STYLE

Look at the way Henry uses **alliteration** to emphasize Scots aggression: *fullness of his force* (line 150). ✪ Can you find more examples in lines 151–2? ✪ Why does Westmorland describe England as an *eagle* and Scotland as a *weasel*? What impression does he try to give of each country?

The language used by Ely and Exeter in lines 115–24 is emotive (it appeals to the emotions): *these valiant dead/ You are their heir/ blood and courage/ Ripe for exploits and mighty enterprises/ Your brother kings ... expect that you should rouse yourself/ lions of your blood.* In other words, remember your brave ancestors, don't let them down, prove that you are a man and fight like the lions they once were.

21

# HENRY V

### Hotspot

**(Answers on p. 69)**

1 What do you think of Henry so far? Remember – people are often a mixture of qualities! Choose words from the list that you think suit him best:

   kind  stern  ruthless  fair  noble  gentle  brave  cowardly  thoughtful  impulsive  determined.

2 Find a quotation to fit each word you chose for (1).

3 Why is the word *lion* used by both Canterbury and Exeter to describe Henry's ancestors? How are they trying to make Henry feel?

4 Make a list of all the different jobs that Canterbury describes in his speech from lines 190–204 (ending with the words *lazy yawning drone*).

*Don't declare war on your brain. Take a break now.*

## Act 2, The Chorus

The Chorus explains to the audience what will happen in the next Act.

### SUMMARY

◆ Englishmen prepare for war.
◆ The French have bribed three English noblemen to kill the King.
◆ The play will move to Southampton, before the army sails to France.

## War fever

The country is gearing up for war. Young men are leaving their fashionable lives behind. *Honour's thought/ Reigns solely in the breast of every man.* War is a serious and expensive

COMMENTARY

business; the armourers are busy, while many men sell land to equip themselves. Despite the excitement and patriotism, there is a dark side to all this. A terrible plot will be exposed – an attempt to kill the King.

### A word from Will

England did not have a regular army of professional soldiers in Henry's day. Whenever there was a war, the nobles raised their own companies of men ready to fight. The nobles often paid for their own horses and equipment. They did this to support the King, who would (they hoped!) look upon them kindly and grant them more favours and titles when the war was over.

## STYLE

The language used here is patriotic and romantic about England and the King. Look at the way Henry is described: *the mirror of all Christian kings.* He is the ideal, perfect king. England is described as a *little body with a mighty heart*, making England sound small and brave. Shakespeare describes Henry's subjects as England's *children,* so that the kingdom sounds like a happy family. The mention of the plot to kill the King sounds a darker note however. The Chorus gives the audience a sense of where each scene will be set: *Southampton …/ And thence to France shall we convey you safe.*

### Act 2, scene 1: *We meet some of Henry's rowdy old friends*

**Setting:** The Boar's Head Tavern, London.

Compared to a pub of today, the inn will be dirty and dark. The characters will be scruffy – they are poor, unlike the noblemen we have seen previously.

23

# HENRY V

> **A word from Will**
>
> I like to give some of my characters names that fit their personalities. It gives audiences useful clues and makes them laugh. In my day *Nym* was a slang word for 'thief', and *Pistol* was a hand gun. Mistress *Quickly* suggests how she dealt with clients when she worked at her old trade as a prostitute, before marrying Pistol of course!

### *SUMMARY*

- ◆ Bardolph, Pistol and Nym prepare for the war.
- ◆ Pistol and Nym quarrel over Mistress Quickly's affections.
- ◆ The men's old master, Sir John Falstaff, is ill.
- ◆ Nell returns with news: Falstaff's illness is very serious.

## Dramatic contrast

This scene uses **comic relief** to make the audience laugh after the solemn atmosphere in the council chamber and the talk of war. (Note: Mistress Quickly is the landlady of the tavern. She is also called Nell or the Hostess.)

## Boasters

Nym is jealous because the Hostess married Pistol. She used to be Nym's girlfriend. Bardolph tries to make peace. Luckily the two rivals are 'all mouth' and just issue lots of threats! ✪ Do you think they are the sort of characters that are likely to act more bravely when they have to fight in France?

## Insults

Practise saying these expressions in the most aggressive and exaggerated way you can:

*Pish for thee, Iceland dog/ shog off/ egregious dog/ o viper vile/ o braggart vile.*

# COMMENTARY

> **A word from Will**
>
> We Elizabethans loved good curses and insults! Audiences enjoyed watching these boastful but cowardly men make fools of themselves.

## Sir John is dying

The scene ends with the Hostess coming back in saying that Sir John Falstaff is very sick. He was the leader of this gang of roughnecks when it included Henry before he was King. Henry cut Falstaff dead the moment he gained the throne. The shock of this was the start of Falstaff's illness.

### STYLE

The Hostess is a kind but uneducated woman. She often mixes up her words (using **malapropisms**). When she fears that Pistol will be stabbed by Nym, she cries out: *we shall see wilful adultery and murder committed.* 'Adultery' means being unfaithful to your partner – she means to say 'assault'!

> **Act 2, scene 2:** *The traitors are uncovered and condemned*

Henry makes a difficult decision after he discovers a plot to kill him. He shows himself to be a stern and powerful leader.

**Setting:** Southampton. This was one of the most important ports in England. A director might emphasize its business to contrast with the dark tavern in the previous scene.

### SUMMARY

◆ Henry sets a trap for the traitors, then accuses them.
◆ They are sentenced to death.
◆ Henry is shocked by their betrayal. He trusted them.

## *S*hock and anger

Exeter, Bedford and Westmorland discuss the plot against Henry. They are particularly angry about Scroop's betrayal. He was one of the King's most trusted companions (*bedfellow* means a close friend here).

## *S*uspense

The traitors do not realize that Henry has uncovered their plot. In lines 13–39 he puts the three men at their ease, though he is actually setting a trap for them. They flatter the King, which turns the audience against them even more. Look at how smoothly they talk about him. *Sweet shade of your government* is one phrase used by Cambridge, as if the King's rule is like a beautiful tree giving shelter.

## *P*uns without fun

There are frightening double meanings (**puns**) in Henry's words but Scroop, Cambridge and Gray don't realize it. *The powers we bear with us/ Will cut their passage …/ Doing the execution and the act/ For which we have in head assembled them?* Henry seems to be discussing what the army will do (*execution* means 'carrying out' as well as 'killing'). In fact, he is using the word's second meaning – having traitors' heads cut off!

## *T*hey fail the test

Henry asks Exeter to release a man who was locked up for drunkenly abusing the King, but Scroop argues that the King is too soft. He advises Henry to make an example of him. Henry moves on, apparently giving the three traitors their written instructions for the war. But the papers he hands them are in fact evidence of their crimes. They beg for mercy but he reminds them how hard they were on the drunken man: *The mercy that was quick in us but late/ By your own counsel is suppressed and killed.* (I felt merciful towards you until you spoke out against that man.) ✪ Do you think Henry is truthful here? Look at the threats in his puns earlier in the scene.

COMMENTARY

# These English monsters

Henry is hurt as well as angry. He reminds Cambridge and Gray how he honoured them with privileges. They betrayed him for money, but his friend Scroop's treachery hurts the most. Henry says that Scroop *knew'st the very bottom of my soul*. He then describes them as *monsters ... inhuman*. People in Shakespeare's time believed that real monsters lived in far parts of the world, but here we have *English monsters*.

# Like another fall of man

Henry also uses a Bible story as a way of showing the seriousness of Scroop's betrayal. Adam and Eve were banished from paradise after they disobeyed God. This is called the 'fall of man'. Christians believe that human misery and wickedness came from Adam and Eve's sin. Killing a king was a particularly serious crime in the past.

---

**A word from Will**

Kings and queens had huge power in my day, based on something called the Divine Right of Kings. It was believed that God chose monarchs to rule over ordinary people. Rulers had the power of life and death over their subjects.

---

## KEY IDEAS

There are two key ideas here. First of all, the terrible sin of **killing a king**, secondly, the idea that **appearances** can deceive. The traitors seemed so refined and so good that now they have betrayed him it will be difficult to trust anyone, even if they are perfect: *Such and so finely bolted didst thou seem./ And thus thy fall hath left a kind of blot/ To mark the full fraught man.*

# HENRY V

## *STYLE*

This is a tense scene that uses **dramatic irony**. Shakespeare has already told the audience that Henry knows about the plot, so we are just waiting to see how he will deal with the three men. Everyone is in the know but them.

Henry uses **rhetorical questions** to emphasize how the three traitors fooled everyone. For example: *Seem they grave and learnéd?/ Why, so didst thou.*

### Hotspot

(Answers p. 69)

1 Henry's speech to the traitors beginning, *The mercy that was quick within us but late,* is long. He could condemn them in far fewer words. Why does Henry speak at such length about the plot? What might he be feeling?

2 Are you surprised by the death penalties? What do they reveal about Henry?

3 What was the crime of the man who was *committed yesterday*?

4 Imagine you were a soldier watching the scene. Describe how Henry and the conspirators behaved.

*Exams are not a conspiracy. Grant yourself mercy, take a break.*

### Act 2, scene 3: *War and death*

**Setting:** The Boar's Head Tavern, London.

#### SUMMARY

◆ Nym, Pistol, Bardolph and the Boy prepare to leave for the war.

# COMMENTARY

- They learn about Falstaff's death from Nell Quickly, the Hostess.
- They grieve for their old friend and employer before leaving.

## Arthur's bosom

The Hostess mixes her words again. She describes the destination for Falstaff's soul as *Arthur's bosom* when she really means 'Abraham's bosom', an expression for heaven. But Arthur is a famous mythical English hero, so perhaps Shakespeare is suggesting that an old soldier like Falstaff is going to a good place. ('Bosom' means chest or heart here!)

## Falstaff's final moments

The Hostess speaks tenderly about the old knight. When he becomes feverish, she realizes that he is dying: *after I saw him fumble with the sheets, and play with flowers … I knew there was but one way.* She tries to cheer him up, but his body is *as cold as any stone.*

## No angel

It is clear that although they are all fond of Falstaff, they have no illusions about him. Notice the mention of drink and women! Bardolph seems a little bitter that he did not get paid much by Falstaff: *the fuel* [drink] *is gone … That's all the riches I got in his service.*

## Bleed the French

Pistol says a fond farewell to his wife, the Hostess, and urges on his companions. *Let us to France, like horseleeches, my boys, to suck … the very blood to suck.* (Let's bleed the French dry of all their money.) ✪ Why do you think Shakespeare included Falstaff's death just as the companions are about to go to war?

# HENRY V

## ✒ STYLE

Notice the use of **comic relief** again. Even though Falstaff has died and the men are going to fight in a terrible war, there is a big contrast between the events in this tavern and the tension of the previous scene at Southampton.

It is often said that the best comedy is very close to tragedy. Here we have a touching description of a man's death, and Shakespeare keeps the sadness going even while making us laugh at the things the characters say, such as *a [he] saw a flea upon Bardolph's nose, and said it was a black soul burning in hell.* (Bardolph has a red nose from heavy drinking.)

---

### Act 2, scene 4: *The French prepare for war*

We meet the French nobility for the first time in this scene.

**Setting:** The French king's palace, Rouen.

### SUMMARY

- ◆ King Charles worries about the English invasion.
- ◆ The Dauphin argues with the Constable about Henry's abilities.
- ◆ Henry sends a threatening message to Charles.

## Don't underestimate the English

King Charles of France is no fool. He reminds the Dauphin and the Constable that France has been beaten by England in previous wars. *It fits us then to be as provident/ As fear may teach us, out of late examples/ Left by the fatal and neglected English.* (We must be careful because we fatally underestimated the English in the past.)

## The Dauphin shows off

The Dauphin responds with a scornful attack on Henry: *she* (England) *is so idly kinged,/ Her sceptre so fantastically borne,/*

COMMENTARY

*By a vain, giddy, shallow, humorous youth,/ That fear attends her not.* In other words, Henry is such a hopeless king that there is no reason to fear England. The Constable (a powerful minister in France) tells the Dauphin to be quiet and agrees with Charles about Henry. The Dauphin comes across as a loud-mouthed boaster. He does not want to listen to advice from others.

## Exeter's message

Henry's uncle, the Duke of Exeter, arrives with a threatening message for the French. He gives them the proof that Henry has a claim to the throne and says that Charles must give up the French crown. If he does not, war will follow. Charles promises a reply by the next day.

### KEY IDEAS

The main idea in this scene is that the older statesmen are cautious about war because they know what suffering it causes. The Dauphin is young and boastful and talks about war as if it is a hunt. *Coward dogs/ Most spend their mouths when what they seem to threaten/ Runs far before them.* (Cowardly dogs bark most loudly when the animal they chase is far away.) He boasts to Exeter about the tennis balls joke he played on Henry, but is silent after Exeter puts him in his place: *be assured, you'll find a difference,/ ... That you shall read/ In your own losses.* (You will realize how much Henry has changed when you lose the war.)

✪ Compare the Dauphin's attitude to Henry's. Who is the more realistic about the horrors of war?

The idea of English **patriotism** is also important in this scene. Shakespeare contrasts the just and serious English leaders with the vain and boastful French. You can imagine the 'groundlings', the people who paid a few pennies to watch the play from the yard, jeering at the French. Shakespeare is setting up the 'good' English against the arrogant French.

# HENRY V

## ✎ STYLE

Exeter begins speaking in a formal way (lines 77–96), but changes to a more direct, everyday style from line 98 onwards. He delivers Henry's message in the correct way, polite even though he is talking to enemies. But when Charles asks him what will happen if the French do not obey Henry, he says immediately: *bloody constraint.* (There will be a blood-bath.)

Exeter compares Henry to Jove, king of the gods. In the legends Jove used a thunderbolt as a weapon, so Exeter describes Henry as coming in *fierce tempest .../ In thunder and in earthquake.* ✪ How would you feel if you were the French King and heard this?

Exeter uses **personification**. He makes the war sound like a huge monster waiting to be fed. *This hungry war/ Opens his vasty jaws.* Such a description emphasizes the terror that war brings. The descriptions of the innocent people who will die are meant to remind Charles that Henry will stop at nothing if he has to. ✪ Count how many types of people will die in the war (lines 107–9).

## Act 3, The Chorus

The Chorus explains to the audience what will happen next.

### SUMMARY

◆ The English army leaves for France.
◆ They put the town of Harfleur under siege.
◆ Charles offers his daughter Katherine in marriage but Henry rejects the offer.
◆ The English attack Harfleur with cannons.

The Chorus paints a vivid picture of the army on the move. The ships' flags are so bright that they imitate the rays of the sun: *With silken streamers the young Phoebus feigning.* (Phoebus was the sun god.) The audience is asked to use its imagination again: *suppose that you have seen/ Play with your fancies* [imagination]*/ o do but think you stand upon the rivage* [shore]*/ work, work your thoughts.*

# COMMENTARY

There is a feeling of sadness mixed with the glory. All those men fit enough to fight have left for war, only women, children and old men are left at home.

### Act 3, scene 1: *Go for it, men!*

**Setting:** Outside the city walls of Harfleur.

#### SUMMARY

◆ Henry urges his men to fight fiercely.

## Once more unto the breach, dear friends

This is one of Shakespeare's most famous quotations. The *breach* is the gap that the English have blown in the walls of Harfleur. Old towns were walled to protect them from siege, but Henry's army is trying to break in.

# HENRY V

## ✒ STYLE

Henry uses fierce words to encourage his men to fight. *Imitate the action of the tiger/ Stiffen the sinews, conjure up the blood.* He explains that they must look terrifying to the enemy because it gives them a better chance of winning. The eyes must stare, the forehead frown and the teeth be clenched with the nostrils flaring. *Lend the eye a terrible aspect/ … Let the brow o'erwhelm it …/ Now set the teeth and stretch the nostril wide.* These descriptions remind us more of wild animals than human beings.

### Act 3, scene 2: *Boasters and cowards*

**Setting:** Behind the English front lines at Harfleur.

#### SUMMARY

- ◆ Pistol, Nym and Bardolph hang back, but Captain Llewellyn forces them into battle.
- ◆ The Boy realizes his companions are cowards and thieves. He decides to leave them.

## The Boy feels let down

The Boy is disappointed by the bad example the three cowards have shown him: *I am boy to all three, but all they three … could not be man to me.* He is a young servant, but they don't act like good masters towards him. He uses contrasts to emphasize their bad points.

Bardolph is a coward but looks brave: he is *white-livered and red-faced*. Pistol is 'all mouth' and promises, but does his best to avoid fighting: *he hath a killing tongue and a quiet sword.* Nym says little, but does not do much either, so he is also a coward: *He hath heard that men of few words are the best men … but his few bad words are matched with as few good deeds.*

COMMENTARY

Nym and Bardolph are always stealing and the Boy realizes that they will turn him into a pickpocket if he stays with them. *They would have me as familiar with men's pockets as their gloves or their handkerchiefs.*

## STYLE

The Boy uses clever wordplay to express his disgust. *It is plain pocketing of wrongs* means both putting up with insults and receiving stolen goods. *Their villainy goes against my weak stomach* means that their wickedness makes him feel sick and goes against his principles. *I must cast it up* means that he wants to reject it, and vomit!

### Act 3, scene 3: *Four captains discuss military tactics*

**Setting:** Outside Harfleur, another part of the siege.

### SUMMARY

- Llewellyn is worried about the mining under Harfleur's walls.
- Captains Llewellyn, Gower, Macmorris and Jamy argue about the rules of war.
- Harfleur asks to talk peace.

## Mining

The English army is tunnelling under the walls of Harfleur so that they can break in and take the city. (Tunnels were filled with explosives and set off.) Llewellyn is worried that the tunnels might collapse and kill the soldiers because the mining has been done badly. Another danger is from countermines. The people defending Harfleur will dig their own mines (countermines) under the attacking miners if they see or feel the ground vibrating.

# He *is an ass*

Llewellyn (Welsh) is worried that Macmorris (Irish) is in charge of the mining. He thinks that Macmorris is stupid and inexperienced. Macmorris appears with Jamy (Scottish). Llewellyn wants to discuss military strategy with Macmorris but the Irishman is impatient – there is a battle to be fought. They argue and are ready to fight each other when they hear a parley (a trumpet signalling that Harfleur wants peace talks).

---

**A word from Will**

What you now call the United Kingdom was anything but united in my day. The Irish were at war with the English throne and the Scots were always ready to cross the border into England and fight. I wanted a Captain from every country of the Kingdom to show that most people were united behind Henry in his fight for the throne of France.

---

## STYLE

Writers often use **stereotypes** as a form of humour. National stereotypes are based on what is supposed to be 'typical' of a person from a certain country. A 'typical' Scot is supposed to be mean with money, a 'typical' Irishman is supposed to be stupid. There are jokes like this all around the world. Shakespeare uses some stereotypes that would have been popular with his audience. Notice how he exaggerates accents. Llewellyn says 'look you' a lot. ✪ See if you can identify special words from each country.

---

### Act 3, scene 4: *Surrender!*

Harfleur surrenders because there is no help from the Dauphin.

**Setting:** Outside the walls of Harfleur.

COMMENTARY

### SUMMARY

◆ Henry threatens destruction of the town if the governor does not surrender.
◆ The governor agrees and opens the gates.

## Horror and destruction

Henry shows his ruthless side. He warns the governor that this is Harfleur's last chance to surrender and paints a terrible picture of what will happen if they don't. The English will burn the town and the soldiers will act like murdering gardeners, raping young women and killing babies. He says that it will be the governor's fault if this happens! ✪ Look at lines 36–8 for other threats.

---

**A word from Will**

There's nothing like violence to keep an audience interested. You watch films with lots of gore. We did not have such good special effects, so we got the audience's imagination running wild with our bloodthirsty descriptions.

---

## A small victory

The governor agrees to Henry's conditions, then leaves to break the news to the townsfolk. We learn that Henry's army is weak and sick – but he has still managed to take Harfleur. He orders his uncle, Exeter, to *use mercy to them all*. That is to say, the army must be gentle on the people of the town.

### KEY IDEAS

Although it is clear that Henry will use force and cruelty when necessary, he is not cruel or greedy for the sake of it. ✪ Do you think he means what he says to the governor, or is he trying to frighten him into surrendering and so avoid further deaths on both sides?

# HENRY V

## Act 3, scene 5: *English lessons*

**Setting:** A room in the French king's palace, Rouen.

### SUMMARY

- ◆ Princess Katherine wants to learn English.
- ◆ Alice teaches her words for some parts of the body.
- ◆ Katherine is shocked because some of the words sound rude.

## *More comic relief*

This is a comic scene after Henry's aggressive speech in scene 4. Don't be put off if you do not understand what Katherine says. Most of Shakespeare's audience couldn't speak French either! The young men playing Katherine and Alice would have used mime to help the audience understand what was going on. The humour of the scene is about foreigners trying to learn English and getting it wrong, and also *foot* and *count*, which sound like certain English four-letter words!

## *What's this got to do with the war?*

The scene might seem a bit odd in the middle of a play about war. But as well as providing light relief and contrast, Shakespeare may have been trying to make the play a bit more romantic by introducing Katherine to the audience. (She marries Henry at the end of the play.) It also suggests that the French are not as 'clever' as the English because they don't speak our language!

## Act 3, scene 6: *Get Henry!*

**Setting:** A council chamber at the palace, Rouen.

### SUMMARY

- ◆ The French leaders are shocked by the English army's success.

COMMENTARY

- Charles orders the lords to defeat Henry and take him prisoner.
- The Constable reminds them that the English army is small and weak.

## Norman bastards!

The Norman French invaded England in 1066. The English nobility is therefore a mixture of Anglo-Saxon and Norman blood, which is why Bourbon calls them 'Norman bastards'.

Bourbon and the Dauphin cannot understand how the English can be such brave fighters. The English weather is terrible and they have a disgusting drink – beer! French women are even threatening to sleep with the English because they are so much braver than Frenchmen.

## Bring him our prisoner

The French King makes a decision. He orders the lords to show honour and stop the defeats. (*Now quit you of great shames.*) Most importantly, they must capture Henry.

### KEY IDEAS

The French are again shown as arrogant and dismissive. Shakespeare is raising the stakes before the battles begin. Remember this play is based on actual events, and most of the audience would have known that the English finally won the war.

### STYLE

A lot of the **imagery** in this scene uses weather. The French regard the English as weak and cold-blooded because England is a cold, wet country. (*The sun looks pale,/ Killing their fruit with frowns …/ a more frosty people*).

# HENRY V

> ### Act 3, scene 7: *Bardolph comes to a bad end*

**Setting:** A bridge over the River Ternoise.

### SUMMARY

- Pistol appeals to Llewellyn to save Bardolph's life.
- Llewellyn refuses, so Pistol leaves angrily.
- The English have captured the bridge.
- Henry agrees with Bardolph's death sentence.
- French herald Mountjoy delivers Charles's demand for surrender.
- Henry admits the weakness of his army but is defiant.

## Gallant service

Llewellyn tells Gower how Exeter and Pistol defended the bridge over the river Ternoise. He is full of praise for Pistol: *he is as valiant a man as Mark Antony*. (Mark Antony was a famous Roman hero, so Llewellyn must be very impressed.)

## Do me favours

Pistol enters and asks Llewellyn for help. Bardolph has been arrested for robbing a church and will be hanged if Llewellyn does not put a good word in with Exeter. Llewellyn refuses. Bardolph knew the rules but broke them anyway: *discipline ought to be used*. Pistol makes a rude sign and leaves in a rage.

## An arrant counterfeit rascal

Gower tells Llewellyn the truth about Pistol, that he is absolutely false (*arrant counterfeit*) as well as a pimp and thief (*a bawd, a cutpurse*). Gower says there are many men like Pistol. They join the army occasionally so they can brag about it afterwards, but they are not brave, just boastful. Llewellyn swears revenge on Pistol for making him look a fool.

COMMENTARY

## The duke is a brave man

Llewellyn is full of praise for Exeter for holding the bridge. He tells Henry about Bardolph's crimes. Even though Bardolph and Henry were once friends, the King shows no mercy. He does not want the French people to be mistreated, so Bardolph's death will be a warning to other soldiers. He describes war as a game that is won by the army that shows fairness and kindness when it is appropriate. (*When lenity and cruelty play for a kingdom, the gentler gamester is the soonest winner.*) ✪ Might Henry be quite glad to get rid of his old drinking friends from his wild youth? The dead can't tell stories.

## Mountjoy

The French ambassador arrives and makes a clever speech that emphasizes the weakness of the English side.

## English propaganda

Henry's reply is honest. He admits that the army is smaller and weaker because of sickness. But he cannot help boasting about the worth of his soldiers. *When they were in health, I tell thee herald, I thought upon one pair of English legs did march three Frenchmen.* (I tell you, when they were healthy, one English soldier was worth three French.) He apologizes for boasting, saying that French air has created the fault in him!

## No surrender

Henry finishes the conversation by saying that he is not worth a ransom and his army is weak and sick, but that the French king had better look out anyway. (*My ransom is this frail and worthless trunk [body], my army but a weak and sickly guard. Yet, God before, tell him we will come on through France himself ... if we may pass, we will. If we be hindered, we shall you tawny ground with your red blood discolour.*)

# HENRY V

## ✎ STYLE

Mountjoy uses opposites to show the power of the French. Waiting for the right moment is better than rushing foolishly. (*Advantage is a better soldier than rashness.*)

The King switches from ordinary speech (prose) when talking to Llewellyn, to iambic pentameter when he makes his important speech to Mountjoy.

### Act 3, scene 8: *French boasts*

**Setting:** The French camp near Agincourt, France.

### SUMMARY

- ◆ The French nobles wait impatiently for morning, when the battle will begin.
- ◆ They boast and argue, confident of winning.

## Macho boasting

The Constable brags about his armour, Orléans about his horse. The Dauphin joins in and boasts so much about his horse that the others get bored and make fun. They make dirty jokes about horses and women. For example, a *jade* is both a run-down horse and a prostitute.

## Backbiting

The Constable is rude about the Dauphin when he leaves. The nobles move on to sporting puns about hawking and archery, trying to score against each other. Finally, they mock Henry and his army. Rambures defends them, saying that England breeds brave creatures, like dogs. Orléans does not agree. He says that their mastiffs (fighting dogs) get killed by fighting creatures bigger than them – rather like the English taking on France! ✪ What impressions of the French does Shakespeare want us to have?

# COMMENTARY

### 🗝 KEY IDEAS

Shakespeare can't make the French look too stupid or the victory over them will not be a worthy one for the brave, outnumbered English. For the same reason, he gives us a sense of the French army being very well equipped.

## Act 4, The Chorus

An actor speaks directly to the audience about the next act.

### SUMMARY

◆ The Chorus describes the atmosphere in each camp.
◆ Henry rouses English morale.

## *A*tmosphere

The night before the battle – and afterwards. The French are arrogant and confident, the English hungry and exhausted. The Chorus gives a beautiful description of the night sounds (*creeping murmur*) and sights (*the poring dark ... foul womb of night*). Remember there was no electric light, nor glow from nearby towns. The only light would have been from fires and burning torches. The armies are so close to each other that they can see the other side's fires and shadowy faces. (*Fire answers fire, and through their paly flames/ Each battle sees the other's umbered face.*)

## *N*ervous

Night is usually a time of rest, but here we get the sense of pre-battle tension. The *dreadful note of preparation* describes the sounds of armour being mended, because the noise reminds everyone of the clash of weapons.

# HENRY V

## Opposites

The French feel so strong and confident that they put bets on beating the English. Henry's soldiers are described as *the poor condemnèd English,/ Like sacrifices*. This reminds us that they are likely to die in battle because they are so weak. They *sit patiently … their gesture sad,/ Investing lank-lean cheeks and war-worn coats …/ So many horrid ghosts*. The English sound like animals waiting to be slaughtered. They are half-starved, ragged and exhausted.

## Leadership: A little touch of Harry in the night

The Chorus describes Henry walking round the camp, cheering the tired men. He gives them confidence – and hope. The Chorus emphasizes how inspiring he is. He makes these exhausted men feel strong and important. He *calls them brothers, friends and countrymen*. He acts in a warm and generous way towards them: *A largess universal like the sun/ His liberal eye doth give to everyone,/ Thawing cold fear*.

### Act 4, scene 1: *The King in disguise*

In this long scene Henry learns what ordinary men who have followed him to France really think of him. He is forced to consider difficult questions: his responsibility for his army, the rightness of his cause and the burdens of kingship. It is the closest we get to knowing Henry's deepest thoughts.

**Setting:** The English camp, Agincourt, night.

#### SUMMARY

- It is near dawn and the army is getting ready for the battle.
- The King talks to his brothers Gloucester and Bedford. Although the English are in danger, he says that makes them braver – and justice is on their side.

# COMMENTARY

- ♦ He encourages Sir Thomas Erpingham, a brave old soldier, and borrows his cloak.
- ♦ Pistol does not recognize the King in disguise and challenges him. He is rude to Henry because he thinks he is related to Llewellyn.
- ♦ The King is impressed by Llewellyn's demand for discipline from the troops.
- ♦ Still disguised, Henry discusses the coming battle with Williams and Bates. Williams paints a picture of the suffering caused by war.
- ♦ Henry argues that a king is not responsible for his soldiers' souls. He also says that the King would rather die in battle than be ransomed. Williams does not believe him.
- ♦ Williams challenges the disguised King. They promise to fight after the battle.
- ♦ Henry thinks aloud about how difficult it is being a king, then prays.

## Great danger

It is 25 October, cold and dark. The exhausted English army huddles round its fires, sleeping on the open ground. The enemy camp is so close they can hear the French, *our bad neighbours make us early stirrers*. Henry has to give his troops courage.

The attempt to be upbeat in the face of overwhelming odds is begun by the cheery words of Sir Thomas Erpingham who prefers to share the cold ground of France with Henry than be safe in bed at home because he can say *now lie I like a king*.

The King borrows Erpingham's cloak. Kings and nobles wore distinctive suits of armour so that their soldiers could see them in the chaos of battle. Now Henry is disguised. In the rest of the scene he wanders through the camp talking with various men in the army. Not until after his long **soliloquy** (lines 203–57) is he recognized as the King again.

## Laughter before battle

The first person Henry meets is Pistol. Henry gives his name as *Harry le roi* (French for King) but Pistol doesn't get it. Pistol

# HENRY V

insults Llewellyn and praises the King in a strangely disrespectful way that recalls Henry's wild and now vanished past.

Then Henry overhears Llewellyn scolding Gower for talking too loudly. Good soldiers apparently keep quiet in their camps! Henry thinks the Welshman's professional attitude displays *much care and valour*.

> **A word from Will**
>
> This is a long, tense scene, full of foreboding for what will happen when the battle begins. I needed to bring some humour into it so that the audience didn't get bored! But I still needed to raise the tension as the long night passes. That's why people talk about the dawn coming up: the time for battle is getting nearer.

## Ordinary soldiers

Henry meets three English soldiers. This gives Shakespeare the opportunity for Henry to explain his innermost thoughts and feelings. The soldiers are scared of the approaching day. Henry admits their situation is bad, they are *even as men wrecked upon a sand, that looked to be washed off the next tide*. He stresses the need to keep up morale.

Williams and Bates believe that the King is responsible for the war and for the souls of those who die in it. If the war is not just, they might go to hell. Williams paints a dreadful picture of the aftermath of a battle *when all those legs and arms and heads chopped off ... shall join together at the latter day and cry all 'We died at such a place'*. In other words, the dead will rise up and accuse the King. Of course, they don't realize they are talking to him! ✪ What does Williams imagine the dying to be thinking or doing as they die?

## This world and the next

Henry skilfully argues that the King is not bound to answer *the particular endings of his soldiers*. The soldiers owe their king

# COMMENTARY

allegiance, but they must look after their own souls: *Every subject's duty is the king's, but every subject's soul is his own.* Henry is making a distinction between the duty men have in this world to their king, and the duty they have to their own souls. He advises that every soldier should confess his sins before battle, so that if he dies he will be in a state of grace (free of sins) and go to heaven.

### A word from Will

I was taking a bit of a risk here. By painting such a bloody picture, I might have made some people think that the battle really wasn't worth it. But I knew that most of my audience believed in their country no matter what. The real Henry V was a great national hero. Williams' speech adds tension as the time for the battle creeps closer!

# HENRY V

## Ransom

Bates agrees that if he dies the king *should not answer for me, and yet I determine to fight lustily for him*. But of the three soldiers, Williams is the most questioning. When Henry says that the King will not be ransomed, Williams is cynical. If an army was defeated, the common soldiers were taken prisoner or killed, but the nobles were held to ransom, usually treated fairly well and usually ended up back home once the ransom had been paid. Williams says that if he is killed, how will he know whether the king keeps his word?

This leads to an argument between Henry and Williams which they agree to settle if they survive the battle. They exchange gloves so that they can recognize one another again. ✪ How angry do they seem with one another?

## Left alone

In his long soliloquy Henry reflects on the difficulties of being a king. He thinks all the pomp and ceremony is worthless. He compares this long night, and other sleepless nights that the burdens of kingship bring, to the easy sleep of the *wretched slave*, the simple labourer who every night *sleeps in Elysium* (paradise). Henry envies the labourer, who he thinks has *the forehand and vantage of a king*.

✪ If you were directing an actor to give this speech, what tone would you want them to adopt? Is Henry really despairing, or is he accepting his heavy burden of kingship? Make a few notes that you could give to the actor.

## A prayer

Before he goes off to meet his nobles, Henry prays for his outnumbered men. He begs God not to let him suffer now for *the fault my father made in compassing the crown* from Richard II. (Historical note: Henry's father fought Richard II for the English throne and had the deposed king put in prison, where he died, probably murdered. Henry feels God may punish him for what his father did.)

# COMMENTARY

## STYLE

Notice that throughout his long debate with the soldiers Henry speaks in prose, the language of ordinary characters. This shows that he can 'come down to their level' while still putting forward complex arguments. But when they leave him he returns to blank verse, even though he is actually talking to himself! He is returning to his role as a king.

The scene ends with a **rhyming couplet** (pair of rhyming lines). This device is used to end many scenes in the play. It lets the audience know that the scene is about to change.

### Hotspot

**(Answers on p. 69)**

1 What do you learn of Henry in this scene? Choose words to describe him:
   kind  ruthless  thoughtful  hopeful  brave  cowardly despairing  clever  determined.

2 Write a line describing Henry's mood at the end of the scene.

3 When Henry is talking with Williams (lines 134–68), what sins does he list that soldiers might have already committed?

4 Describe how Henry might think of each of these characters before the battle: Erpingham, Pistol, Llewellyn, Bates.

*Take a break before taking on the French army.*

# HENRY V

### Act 4, scene 2: *Confident French*

**Setting:** The French camp near Agincourt.

#### SUMMARY

- ◆ The French nobles confidently prepare for battle.
- ◆ They joke about how weak the English are.
- ◆ Grandpré and Bourbon joke about how ragged the English are.
- ◆ The French cannot wait to go to battle.

## First light

A messenger tells the French nobles and the Constable that the English are *embattled,* in position to fight. The French arrogantly think that the English will be defeated so quickly that there will not be *work enough for all our hands.*

COMMENTARY

# A *hilding foe*

The French describe the poor condition of Henry's army, a *hilding* (worthless) foe. They think there will be not enough blood in the English to stain all the French swords. Grandpré encourages the French nobles to get ready to fight. He describes the English war horses as *poor jades* over which the crows who feed on the dead after battles fly impatiently. The Dauphin jokes that maybe the French should feed and clothe the English.

### Act 4, scene 3: *Brave faces*

**Setting:** The English camp near Agincourt.

#### SUMMARY

- ◆ The English nobles put on a brave face about being outnumbered.
- ◆ Henry argues that if there were more soldiers, they would have to share the honour of victory.
- ◆ Henry says any soldier who wants to leave may do so.
- ◆ Henry makes the 'Saint Crispin's Day' speech to rally the troops.
- ◆ Mountjoy gives Henry a last chance to put himself up for ransom and spare his soldiers.
- ◆ Henry refuses. He tells Mountjoy that the English are weakened but still to be feared.

# *Raising the tension*

The battle of Agincourt is the dramatic high point of the play. The last few scenes have been building up to it. Now we learn that the French outnumber the English by five to one. Nonetheless the English nobles vow to fight valiantly.

# HENRY V

## More honour for us

The King is now completely 'in role' as the great leader. He has to raise his army's spirits one last time.

Henry gives a great rousing speech to the troops (lines 18–67). It is one of the best-known speeches in any Shakespeare play. He begins by saying that he would not want any more troops because if there were more soldiers, they would have to share the honour with them when the French are defeated. Shakespeare needs this heroic king to be the embodiment of honour, and Henry says *But if it be a sin to covet honour,/ I am the most offending soul alive.*

## Leave now if you want

Henry shows his generosity by proclaiming that any man who does not want to fight may leave now: *his passport shall be made,/ And crowns for convoy* [money to get home] *put into his purse.* Most kings would be more likely to kill anyone trying to avoid the fight! ✪ What impression of Henry is Shakespeare trying to create here?

## St Crispin's Day

The most famous section of this long speech begins when Henry says that today, 25 October, is the Feast of St Crispian (also known as Crispin) – a public holiday in England.

Henry's brilliant and moving speech builds to a climax. Imagine the troops cheering at the end, roused by his words. The King paints a picture of the soldiers who will fight today as old men showing their scars proudly. Notice how this suggests that they will survive. Their names will be remembered for ever, *And Crispin Crispian shall ne're go by/ From this day to the ending of the world/ But we in it shall be remembered.* He uses *we* here to emphasize that they are all together as brothers in the battle.

On stage this great speech is usually greeted by a cheer from the soldiers gathered round listening.

## COMMENTARY

> ### A word from Will
>
> I've built up the pre-battle tension to its peak here. Remember that in Henry's time, and my own, battles were 'set-pieces'. There were rules of war. Basically the two armies picked a spot to fight, lined up and charged. After that, deadly hand-to-hand fighting began. Some men in my audience might have first-hand experience of waiting for a battle like Agincourt to begin.

## One last chance

Mountjoy, the French herald comes to the English camp to ask if Henry will surrender and be ransomed. Of course Henry refuses. He tells Mountjoy that his men may look ragged, but they do not lack courage.

### KEY IDEAS

Henry brilliantly plays on the **patriotic** idea of being English and of gaining fame as an English fighter.

In Act 4, scene 1 Henry prayed that God might look kindly on his army. He ends his speech to Mountjoy with another appeal to God. Shakespeare is underlining Henry's **religious beliefs**, his hope that God will smile on the English. The scene ends with another prayer.

### STYLE

Only nobles feature in this scene, though we imagine ordinary soldiers gathered round Henry, so it is all written in blank verse. Henry's St Crispin's Day speech is highly poetic. He paints a vivid picture of his soldiers as old men and he uses highly emotive language to glorify their cause: *We few, we happy few, we band of brothers.*

Notice the rhyming couplet used to close the scene.

# HENRY V

## Hotspot

**(Answers on p. 69)**

1 Imagine you were a soldier listening to Henry encouraging you to fight. In a few lines explain what he said.

2 Who:
   (a) is *Not covetous of gold*?
   (b) *Will stand a tiptoe when this day is named*?
   (c) *Shall think themselves accursed they were not here*?
   (d) *Will with all expedience charge on us*?
   (e) *shall breed a plague in France*?

3 What could Henry's aside after Mountjoy has left – *I fear thou wilt once more come again for ransom* – reveal about the King's thoughts?

*Be fresh for the battle — take a break.*

---

### A word from Will: Staging the battle

The next four scenes take place in quick succession on different parts of the field. I only had a small stage, a dozen or so actors and no special effects except 'chambers' (fireworks) to create the battle. So I've written 'snapshots' of events and reports of the main battle. You have to imagine the thousands of men fighting, the cavalry charges and the slaughter. My audience knew nothing of special effects, but they were good at using their imaginations.

---

On the day of the actual battle of Agincourt, the French had 30,000 men, many on fresh war horses. The English had just 900 men-at-arms, who would fight with sword and pike. But Henry had 6,000 highly skilled archers. Their showers of arrows destroyed the French cavalry, who got bogged down in the mud. Shakespeare claims that at the end of the day 10,000 French lay dead, while on the English side only four nobles and 25 common soldiers died. He lists them in Act 4, scene 8. In fact, historians say only 7,000 French died, and about 200 English.

# COMMENTARY

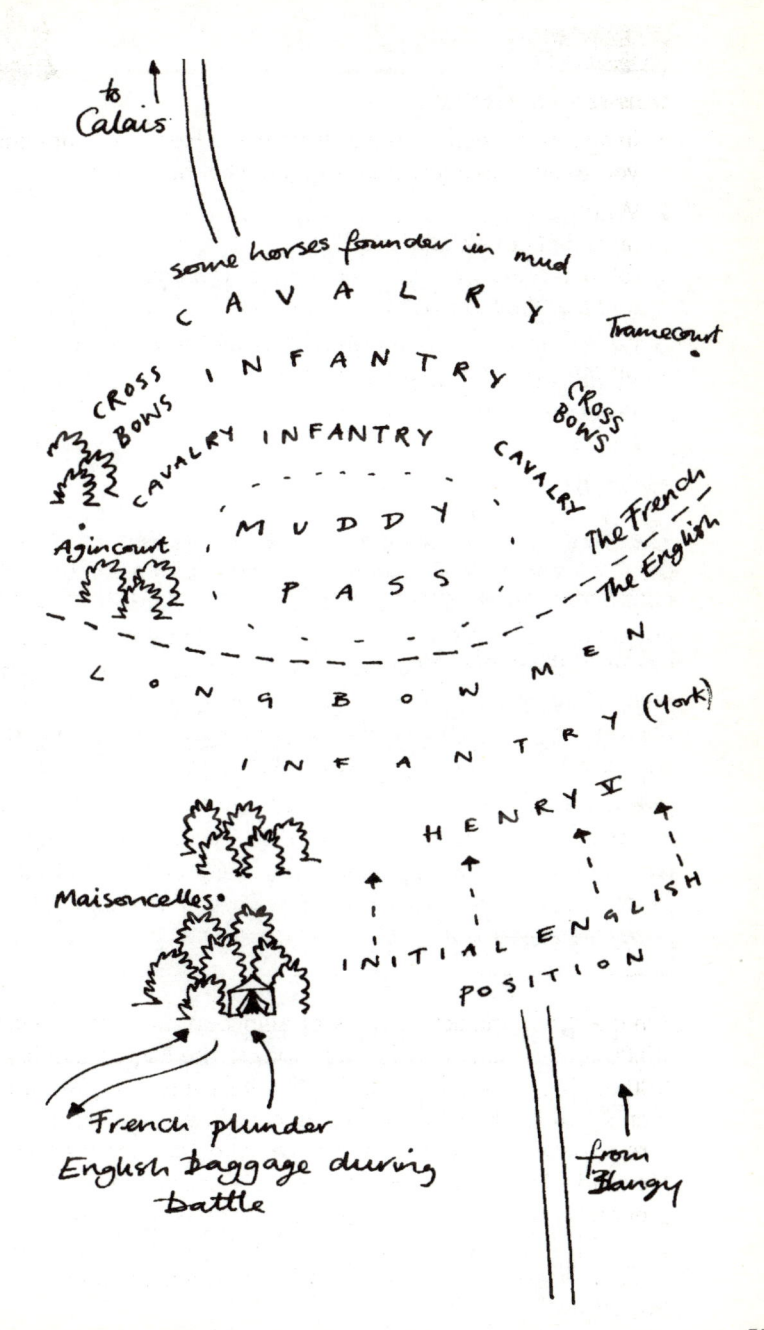

# HENRY V

## Act 4, scene 4: *All mouth*

**Setting:** Agincourt battlefield.

### SUMMARY

- Pistol has taken a French lord prisoner.
- The Boy has to translate for the two men.
- Pistol makes lots of threats before agreeing to a ransom of two hundred crowns.
- The boy is disgusted at Pistol's cowardice. He says Pistol is all talk – even Bardolph and Nym were braver and they have been hanged.

## A *ransom*

After all the tension and drama of the preparations for battle, the first scene on the battlefield is comic. Pistol has captured a French lord. He threatens to cut the prisoner's throat if he is not given a huge ransom. The Boy tries to translate Pistol's threats and colourful language. After much confusion the Frenchman agrees to a ransom of two hundred crowns. ✪ Do you think Shakespeare's audience understood the Frenchman's speeches? What would their reaction be to the Frenchman?

In his **soliloquy**, the Boy condemns Pistol for being all talk, *the empty vessel makes the greatest sound*. He says that his other old companions, Bardolph and Nym, were braver than Pistol. But they have been hanged. The Boy goes off to guard the army's luggage.

## Act 4, scene 5: *Death or glory!*

**Setting:** Agincourt battlefield.

### SUMMARY

- The French nobles panic – they are losing the battle.
- They lead a last desperate charge.

COMMENTARY

# Defeat

The French army is in disarray. Shakespeare needs to show how terrified they are of the English, but he must not make them too cowardly or the victory will seem too easily won. So the short scene ends with the French lords preparing to mount a last desperate 'do or die' charge. They are hoping to die with honour rather than live with shame.

> ### Act 4, scene 6: *It's not over yet*

**Setting:** Another part of the battlefield.

### SUMMARY

◆ The King praises his soldiers but tells them they haven't won yet.
◆ Exeter tells Henry about the brave deaths of York and Suffolk.
◆ Henry orders all French prisoners to be killed.

# York and Suffolk

The action has jumped swiftly back to the English army. Henry praises his soldiers' successes so far, but warns them that *the French yet keep the field*: they have not turned and fled or surrendered.

Exeter paints a vivid picture of the heroic deaths of York and Suffolk. Seeing York dying, the mortally wounded Suffolk cried out to him, *My soul shall thine keep company to heaven.* They died together, side by side. ✪ What effect is this scene of the dying lords likely to have on the audience?

When Henry hears the French have reinforced their scattered men he orders his army to kill all prisoners. It shows a ruthless side of Henry's nature that only rarely surfaces, but when it does it shows he is capable of ordering terrible savagery. ✪ Do you see him as cruel, or is he just doing what is necessary?

# HENRY V

> **Act 4, scene 7:** *Tragedy before victory –
> and a practical joke*

**Setting:** Another part of the battlefield.

### SUMMARY

- Llewellyn is furious because the French have killed the luggage boys.
- Llewellyn and Gower compare Henry to Alexander the Great.
- Llewellyn mentions Falstaff's death.
- Henry, enraged by the killing of the boys, vows to show no mercy.
- Mountjoy arrives to ask if the French can collect their dead. The English have won.
- Llewellyn is pleased that Henry has Welsh blood.
- Henry gives Williams' glove to Llewellyn and tells him that its owner is a traitor.

## Breaking the rules of war

In the previous scene we saw the English nobles on the battlefield. Now we switch back to the ordinary troops. Llewellyn, the professional soldier, is furious that the French have slaughtered the boys who were guarding the English army's baggage train – *'Tis expressly against the law of arms*. Presumably the Boy has been killed.

Llewellyn compares Henry to the Ancient Greek leader Alexander the Great. After some comic confusion of the Welshman's pronouncing of *Big* as *Pig*, the humour continues when the proud Llewellyn tries to compare Henry's birthplace, the Welsh market town of Monmouth, with the legendary Greek city of Macedon.

## More throat-slitting

Henry breaks up the conversation that has drifted far from the battle when he arrives, furious at the slaughter of the boys. He has seen some French knights still grouped on a hill; they must

# COMMENTARY

flee or fight. And he again says that the prisoners will be killed, by having their throats cut.

## You've won

Mountjoy comes to ask if the French *may wander o'er this bloody field/ To book our dead, and then to bury them.* We imagine that the fighting is now mostly over, and that corpses and dying men lie all across the field of battle. Henry does not know if the English have won, but Mountjoy tells him *The day is yours.* The French are surrendering.

## Leeks and gloves

Tension is now draining from events. The battle is over. Henry and Llewellyn, who are countrymen by birth, speak of the tradition of wearing a leek in your cap on *St Tavy's Day* (St David, patron saint of Wales).

## A glove in your hat?

Williams the soldier arrives, still wearing in his hat the glove Henry gave him when they quarrelled the night before. Henry pretends he knows nothing about this. He asks Llewellyn if such a challenge ought to be honoured. Llewellyn thinks a challenge should always be met. Henry agrees, and sends Williams off with a message.

Henry now has some fun. He gives Williams' glove to Llewellyn, telling him that the glove belonged to Alencon, a brave French knight. Any man that challenges Llewellyn when he sees the glove must be a traitor. He then worries that a fight might break out between Williams and Llewellyn, so sends some lords to stop any trouble.

✪ What do you think of this business with the gloves – and of a king who can order prisoners to be slaughtered one minute and play silly jokes the next?

# HENRY V

> **A word from Will**
>
> I needed to wind down the tension after the battle. I wanted to show the human side of Henry, so I set up this idea of the joke with the gloves. The play can't end here, although the victory is the biggest event in the story.
>
> Henry has to go on and meet his future bride, Katherine, the French princess. The whole idea of marrying Katherine might be political rather than romantic (it will create an alliance between England and France) but again I needed my audience to relate to Henry as an 'ordinary' man after all this fighting. Act 5, scene 2 is the first time in ages that we have seen him out of battle armour!

## Act 4, scene 8: *Mistaken identity*

**Setting:** Another part of the battlefield.

### SUMMARY

- Williams and Llewellyn square up for a fight, but Henry and some lords break it up.
- Henry reveals that it was his glove. After threatening to punish Williams, he pardons and rewards him.
- A herald brings news of the French dead.
- The English have lost only 25 men and 4 noblemen.
- They will sing hymns of praise and bury their dead before leaving for home.

# A *joke* ...

Llewellyn catches up with Williams. They are soon quarrelling. Henry and other lords arrive just in time to stop a fight. Henry admits that it was he Williams quarrelled with last night. Williams apologizes and Henry orders Williams' glove to be filled with crowns (coins). Llewellyn adds a comic touch by putting *a shilling* (5 pence) in as well. A shilling was worth

# COMMENTARY

quite a lot in 1415, but it is nothing compared to the King's gift. Henry recognizes Williams to be a loyal and brave fighter.

## And a serious bit

A herald brings details of the dead and the captured. There is a long list of captured French nobles and *Of other lords and barons, knights and squires,/ Full fifteen hundred, besides common men.* Shakespeare doesn't say whether their throats have yet been cut! Ten thousand French lie dead. In effect the French ruling class has been almost wiped out. The herald's account of French losses runs for nearly thirty lines.

By contrast the report of English losses runs to just three and a half lines: four nobles *and of all other men/ But five and twenty.* ✪ What impression is this contrast trying to create?

The scene ends with the King ordering prayers for the dead and for the army to march for Calais and home.

### Act 5, Chorus: *Moving swiftly on*

#### SUMMARY

- ◆ Once again, the Chorus asks the audience to forgive the play's limitations.
- ◆ He describes Henry's return to London.
- ◆ A summary of the political wheeling and dealing between England and France.
- ◆ The play returns to France five years later.

After once more apologizing, the Chorus runs quickly through events after the battle. The audience must imagine the battered but victorious army marching to Calais, landing on the *English beach* where they are greeted by *wives, and boys/ Whose shouts and claps out-voice the deep-mouthed sea.* Then he describes the King's triumphant arrival in London.

Finally there is a 'fast-forward' of events, from 1415 to 1420. Several years of political negotiation between France and England are glossed over before the scene returns to France. This time Henry has come to court Katherine, not to make war.

# HENRY V

## Act 5, scene 1: *Welsh revenge*

**Setting:** The English camp.

### SUMMARY

- Llewellyn promises Gower that he will pay Pistol back for mocking his leek.
- Llewellyn gets his revenge on Pistol.
- Pistol learns that his lover is dead – he plans to become a *bawd* (a pimp) and thief.

---

**A word from Will**

It might seem strange that Llewellyn, Gower and especially the disreputable Pistol have come back to France with Henry after several years have passed since Agincourt. But I did not want to introduce new characters so close to the end of the play. And Pistol has to be paid back for all his boasting!

---

## Vegetables

This is a rather contrived scene, designed to bring a last comic element into the play before the long final scene where 'everything is wrapped up'. Apparently Pistol found Llewellyn on his own the day before, and insulted him by offering him bread and salt with which to eat the leek which the Welshman wore in his hat. (The leek is the symbol of Wales.) Now Llewellyn plans revenge.

Right on cue Pistol swaggers on. Llewellyn beats Pistol and then makes him eat the raw leek: *By Chesue, I will make him eat some part of my leek, or I will peat* [beat] *his pate* [head] *four days.* Pistol gives in.

# COMMENTARY

> **A word from Will**
>
> Actors invent actions to accompany the words I give them. This is called 'business'. There should be a lot of comic business in this scene as the beaten Pistol has the raw leek rammed into his mouth! He must crave mercy from the triumphant Llewellyn. ✪ Imagine you were helping out at a rehearsal. What advice would you give the two actors to help make the scene funny?

## A *coward and a pimp*

Gower spells out Pistol's true nature for the audience: he is a cowardly knave. Left alone, Pistol laments his bad luck, *Doth fortune play the hussy* [prostitute, false woman] *with me now*. He has learnt that his wife has died of a sexually transmitted disease! These two sexual references should prepare us for Pistol's parting idea. His future career will be as a *bawd* (a pimp) and *cutpurse* (thief). Pistol also laments that now he will be homeless.

### STYLE

Notice that although he is a commoner and therefore speaks prose throughout the play, Pistol exits with a rhyming couplet. This device lets us know that he is leaving for good.

### Act 5, scene 2: *A royal union*

**Setting:** The French King's palace at Troyes.

#### SUMMARY

- Henry meets Charles of France to discuss the peace treaty.
- Burgundy speaks of France's need for peace.
- Henry says France will get peace by agreeing to his conditions.

63

# HENRY V

- ◆ The English and French lords leave to discuss the treaty.
- ◆ Henry and Princess Katherine stay behind. Henry declares his love.
- ◆ Katherine is confused. Henry eventually asks her to marry him – and kisses her.
- ◆ Burgundy jokes suggestively about Katherine's modesty.
- ◆ The men return to the peace treaty. King Charles has agreed to all its terms.
- ◆ Charles gives permission for Katherine to marry Henry.

## Time lapse

The play does not make it entirely clear that five years passed between Henry's victory and the signing of the peace of Troyes. Perhaps Shakespeare did not want to make this too clear to the audience in case this last scene seemed too 'tacked on'.

Neither is the connection between Henry and Katherine fully worked through. He was offered her as a bride during the war. She would have been a sort of trophy. He refused. Now he appears to be coming to her to ask for her hand in marriage, at the same time as sorting out the peace treaty. Is she part of the treaty, or is his courting of her a purely private affair?

## A *solemn occasion*

The mood of this scene echoes the meeting of English lords and clergy at the start of the play. Things have come full circle: the war they were planning then has led them to victory. Though they are defeated, the French lords are gracious to the English.

Burgundy gives a long speech comparing the order and fertility of a France at peace with the destruction war has caused, *Her vine, the merry cheerer of the heart,/ Unpruned, dies.*

## Peace at a price

Henry replies simply to Burgundy's long poetic vision of the damage war does. If the French want peace, they must agree to his conditions. All the lords from both sides go off to work

# COMMENTARY

out the details. Henry is left alone with Katherine and Alice.
✪ Do you think it odd that Henry does not take part in the details of the peace treaty?

> **A word from Will**
>
> After playing the warlike king for so long, I needed Henry to show a more human side now. He is a hero, but also a man. I could imagine my audience thinking 'Can he win a woman's heart like he can a battle?'

## Do you like me Kate?

Henry begins to court Katherine. Marriages were often arranged between great families in Henry's time, and no one usually bothered to ask the woman what she thought of her future husband! So there is tension in this scene. Henry could just demand her as part of the spoils of victory, but Shakespeare needs to show Henry as gentle and caring. So when he says *Do you like me Kate?* he sounds almost humble.

## Pardonnez-moi

Katherine's bad English causes some confusion, but actors usually play the meeting between Henry and his bride with gentle humour, not for out-and-out comic effect.

Henry declares his love, and asks her how she feels about him, though he does seem to see the marriage as a transaction, *Give me your answer, I'faith do, and so clap hands and a bargain.* But he is not demanding her hand in marriage as part of an agreed peace deal.

He says he is not good at the ways of courtship and that he speaks like a *plain soldier*, but he claims his simple virtues will be true and lasting. After a long discussion, in which Henry does almost all the talking, he asks Katherine to marry him.
✪ How do you think Katherine responds to Henry's long speeches from line 104 to his proposal at line 223? Does she reveal that her feelings change?

# HENRY V

## A kiss

Katherine says her father will have to approve the marriage. Henry is confident that he will and tries to kiss her hand. She is shocked – this is not the French way. So Henry kisses her on the lips instead, which is far more shocking!

## Burgundy's a lad!

The lords and the French king return from their discussions. Burgundy makes suggestive jokes about Katherine's modesty.
✪ How do you think Henry would have responded to such comments earlier in the play? What might have caused the change in his attitude?

## A happy ending?

King Charles agrees to Henry's political demands and to his marriage to Katherine. Henry is to be named heir to the French throne.

### KEY IDEAS

Shakespeare wants to show us the human, light-hearted and even loving side to Henry's character. Although he comes to Troyes as a victorious king, he behaves much more like a plain man in this scene than at any other time in the play. It is almost a 'happy ever after' ending.

### STYLE

Notice that when alone with Kate, Henry swaps from 'noble' poetry to prose, creating a sense of easy conversation rather than formal speech-making.

COMMENTARY

## Act 5, scene 3: *Epilogue: The Chorus has the last word*

Despite everything working out for Henry in the previous scene, the Chorus ends the play with a sour note. He jumps forward in time and tells the audience that in the reign of Henry's son England lost the throne of France, *and made his England bleed* (because England was plunged into civil war).

### A word from Will

In some ways it's a shame to end a play designed to stir up feelings of pride and excitement with 'bad news', but this is a history play. It must follow the facts. Most of my audience would have known what happened after Henry's victory and marriage. And although I could have left everything at a point when the future looked good, I wanted to suggest that even kings cannot control fate and the future. Poor Henry fought so hard for peace, but died still leading an army in a war.

## Historical note

Henry married Katherine in June 1420. The Dauphin rejected the peace treaty with England. War continued. Henry died of 'camp fever' (dysentery) in France in 1422, aged 34.

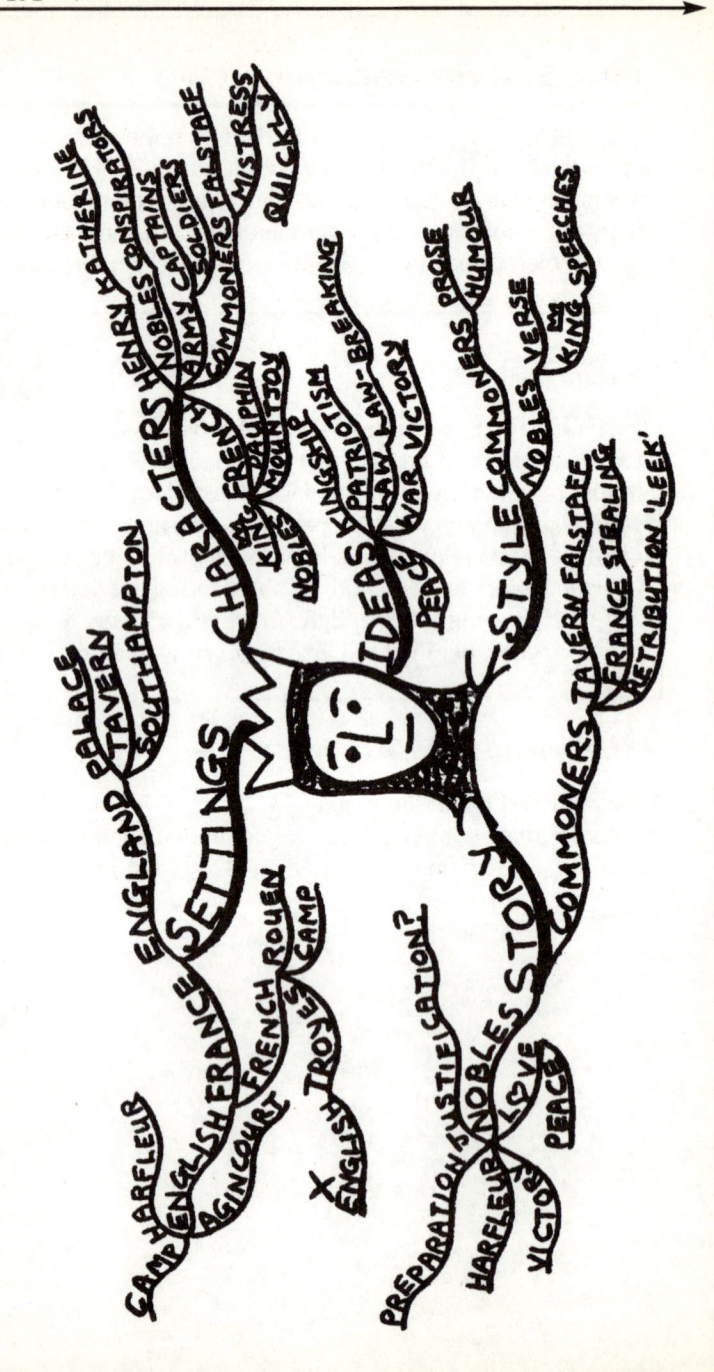

# HENRY V

# COMMENTARY

# Answers to Hotspots

### ACT 1, SCENE 2

**2** Canterbury and Exeter are trying to make Henry feel that he comes from a family of men who were brave fighters.

**3** *magistrates, merchants, soldiers, masons, civil citizens* (ordinary people) and *porters,*

### ACT 2, SCENE 2

**3** He drunkenly abused (*railed against*) the King.

### ACT 4, SCENE 1

**1** Planned (*premeditated*) murders, broken promises of marriage, pillage and robbery.

### ACT 4, SCENE 3

**2** (a) Henry; (b) *The men who fought today*; (c) *gentlemen in England, now abed*; (d) The French; (e) *The dead English who will be buried in France.*

# MODEL ANSWER

## QUESTION

How would you direct a performance of this scene to draw the maximum drama out of the writing?

This is an example of a **dramatic** question (see 'Hints on the Shakespeare exam', p. 75). Before you begin to write you should think about:

- The setting, including possible props.
- How the characters can move about the stage.
- Their body language and any special actions you would write in.
- Relating their actions to the text.
- Identifying the main dramatic points and changes in the scene.
- How characters appear, and what they may really be thinking or feeling.
- Identifying key lines in the scene.

## PLAN

- The drama of the scene and its place in the story.
- Setting the scene.
- King and nobles observed.
- Dramatic tension and irony.
- Henry plays with the conspirators.
- The arrested man.
- The papers are given.
- The King's long speech on loyalty.
- The death sentence.
- Moving on, the bigger picture.

# MODEL ANSWER

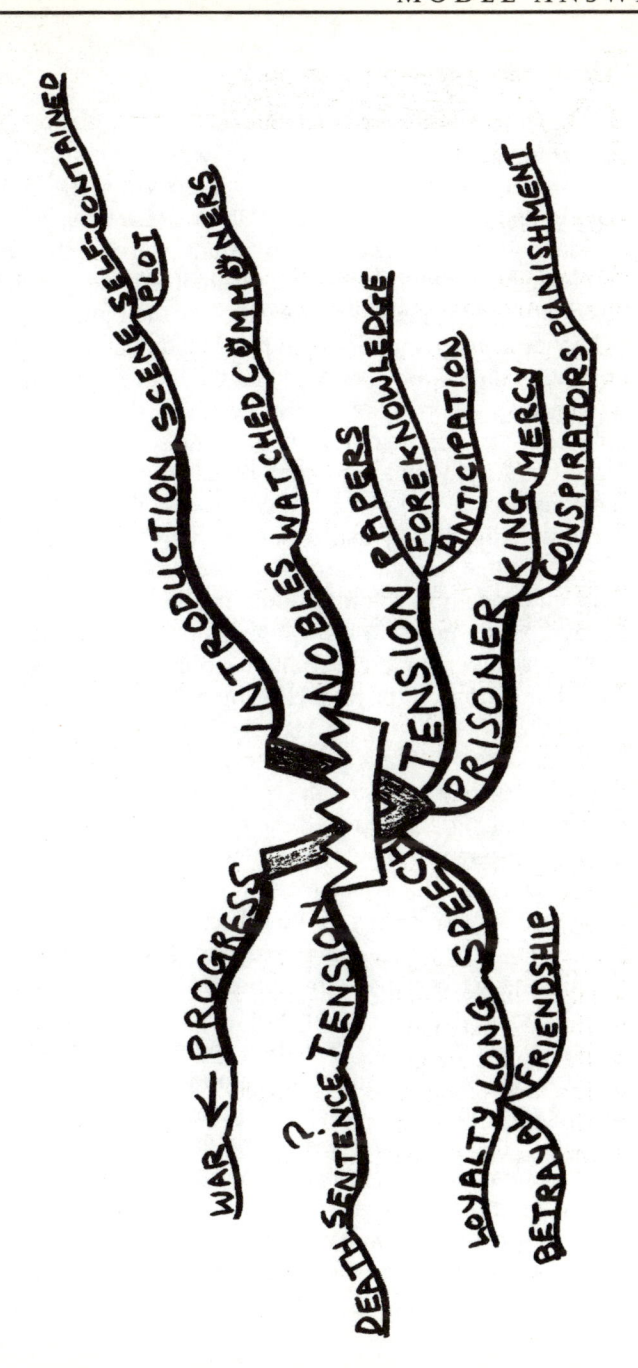

- WAR
- PROGRESS
  - INTRODUCTION
    - SCENE SELF-CONTAINED
    - PLOT
  - NOBLES WATCHED COMMONERS
- ? 
- DEATH SENTENCE TENSION
  - SPEECH
    - PAPERS
    - TENSION
      - FOREKNOWLEDGE
      - ANTICIPATION
    - PRISONER
      - KING MERCY
      - CONSPIRATORS PUNISHMENT
  - LOYALTY LONG
    - BETRAYAL FRIENDSHIP

## THE ESSAY

This scene is a 'self-contained' drama. The conspirators only appear in it, and once they are dealt with their conspiracy is never mentioned again. It is also an important scene in the story in that it tells us a lot about Henry's character. He will do his kingly duty for the good of his country, even if that means condemning a friend (Scroop) to death. It is important that it has drama and impact in a production of the play.[1]

Shakespeare gives the setting just as 'Southampton'. The only other direction we have is that the king is accompanied by 'officers'. We imagine a crowded stage. The army is loading onto boats to take them to France, so the scene probably takes place outdoors, with a sense of movement and crowds. Non-speaking 'extras' can come and go, gradually forming a group about the King as they realize something is going on.[2]

The fact that there are nobles and common men watching must influence how the King, and probably the conspirators, behave. Henry needs to show he is a firm and just king. If he wanted to talk 'man to man' with his old friend Scroop he would only do so in private. Here he must show leadership, however cruel that may be. He tells Scroop, 'The mercy that was quick in us but late/ By your own counsel is suppressed and killed.' (Henry is using the 'royal we', referring to himself in the plural.) Friendship (and the friend) has to be sacrificed.[3]

The conspirators plead but do not grovel for mercy. Honour was a very powerful drive among nobles and they wouldn't want to show fear or beg for their lives in front of the soldiers. What if the King let them live? How could the soldiers respect them?[4] The actors playing the conspirators should balance their terror with a sense of dignity.[5]

All the actors playing the nobles should show they are aware of the officers and soldiers around them, perhaps turning now and again to see if the crowd are listening to their remarks. The King's long speech should be given not just to the conspirators, but to everyone on stage. He is talking as much about himself as a king as about the traitors.[6]

Shakespeare uses dramatic irony of the cruellest kind to create tension in this scene. Often dramatic irony is used to create humour. Everyone in the audience knows something

# MODEL ANSWER

that a character does not know.[7] Here, we know that the King has discovered the conspiracy and when he asks for the conspirators' thoughts on the arrested man, we know they are condemning themselves to be judged as they are judging him.[8]

Three lords open the scene, discussing the conspiracy. They are off to war, and this might be the first time we see them dressed in armour and carrying weapons. It sets a new mood for the play.[9] Within a few lines Henry, the conspirators and other soldiers have arrived. Henry pretends to trust the conspirators, asking them if they think the army is strong enough 'to cut their passage through the force of France,/ Doing the execution and the act/ For which we have in head assembled them.'[10] The use of the word 'execution', meaning here 'to do', must make the audience sit up. Does Henry have execution of another kind on his mind?[11]

Henry lets the conspirators run on. Shakespeare is building the tension here. They must appear absolutely unaware that Henry might suspect them. When Scroop promises 'To do your grace incessant services', he should bow and appear the perfect loyal soldier.[12]

Henry continues to build the tension. The actor playing him could introduce the idea of the arrested man quite lightly, as if it is a small matter about which he is casually asking Scroop's opinion. When all three conspirators have said that Henry is too merciful in suggesting the man be released, he hands out the papers. This is the point where the mood changes. The conspirators read, and look more and more shocked.[13] They make a short appeal for mercy, but now Henry holds the stage. From line 76 to line 141 he speaks uninterrupted. He is the focus of the scene.[14]

Henry's speech is a passionate but well-argued piece of poetry. He should not become angry, but sound more and more powerful. There is no way that the conspirators could dare to interrupt, or contradict him as they did a few minutes before when discussing the prisoner.[15] He reminds Cambridge and Gray how he gave them honours. They are 'English monsters'. But Scroop is worse. He has betrayed not only his king but his friend. Scroop is 'cruel,/ Ingrateful, savage and inhuman'. Henry must put force and hatred into these words, but still keep his kingly dignity.[16]

# HENRY V

When the king has finished, Exeter must read out the full sentences one by one in the voice of a severe judge. Henry's poetry is over, but the tension is not. They are arrested, but they don't yet know the punishment.

Each man makes a speech of apology, perhaps looking to the crowd around them. They come close to begging, but are forced to retain their dignity. They may kneel, but they shouldn't grovel. Henry tells them the sentence is death.

After the conspirators are led away, Henry makes a quick speech to everyone on stage, to his army. He wants to sound a happier note after the events we have just seen. However hurt he is inside, he will not show it to his soldiers and his subjects.

## WHAT'S SO GOOD ABOUT IT?

1. Understanding of how the scene fits into the whole play.
2. Ability to imagine the scene on stage.
3. Understanding of how characters would behave in their social world.
4. Understanding of important background concepts, like honour.
5. Insight into how actors should play the roles.
6. In-depth understanding of Henry's character.
7. Understanding of ideas of dramatic structure.
8. Understanding of how dramatic structure is used in this scene.
9. Good ideas about staging.
10. Good selection of quotes.
11. Good analysis of text.

12–13 Awareness of how acting can bring the text alive.
14–15 Awareness of scene development.
16 Awareness of how lines might be spoken on stage.

# HINTS ON THE SHAKESPEARE EXAM

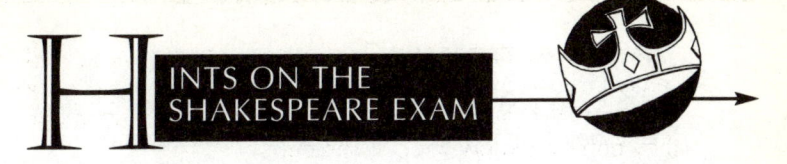

Your SATs Shakespeare exam is 1 hour 15 minutes long. You have to answer **one** task on **one** extract from **one** play. The tasks are of three basic types:

1 **Critical**. *Example:* 'What do you learn about Henry's state of mind from the way he speaks and behaves in this scene?'
2 **Dramatic**. *Example:* 'Imagine you were going to direct Act 1, scene 2 for a performance. What mood would you want to create in the meeting between the bishops and Henry, and how would you have Henry receive the Dauphin's "gift"?'
3 **In character**. *Example:* 'Imagine you are Henry in Act 4, scene 1. Write about your thoughts and feelings as you move through the camp.'

Any one of these types could turn up in the exam.

## THE CRITICAL TASK

The wording of the task is often open-ended, giving you room to express your views and write about what interests you. There are always hints on what to think about, but you may well think of additional ideas.

Stick to the question. You should also stick to the extract – but you will impress the examiner if you show *relevant* knowledge of the whole play. For example you could say how an idea or line echoes one that comes earlier, or hints at what comes later.

You can give your personal response, and it may get you extra marks, but always support it with evidence. Refer to what a character does (e.g. 'Henry borrows Erpingham's cloak') or says (e.g. 'Exeter tells the Dauphin that Henry sends him "scorn and defiance" '), or give a direct quote (e.g. 'When Henry says, "We must bear all" he is revealing his …').

# HENRY V

### *THE DRAMATIC TASK*

For this task you must imagine the play performed on stage. Shakespeare himself gave only very basic **stage directions** (instructions to the actors), so you can use your imagination a lot. However, you should base your suggestions on your understanding of the extract, and give evidence to support your views. For example:

> Henry should not show that he knows the papers being handed to the conspirators are death warrants. They think they are getting instructions for the war. Their faces must slowly change to expressions of shock as they read. They will look to Henry. He will outstare them, like a statue.

### *THE 'IN CHARACTER' TASK*

For this you must imagine you are the character. This can be fun, but you must still base your writing on the evidence. You do not need to write like Shakespeare, but you will get marks for a style that convincingly suggests the character. One good technique is to include short quotations:

> I asked them why they had gone white with fear, why their cheeks were 'paper'. Cambridge was the first to ask for mercy. How dare they! Friends and subjects, they had betrayed me.

Try to feel your way into the part. What do you know about the character? How would he or she think or feel at this point in the play?

### *PLANNING AND CHECKING*

Read the task carefully. If you have studied two extracts, read both tasks and decide which one to do. Then read the extract carefully. Don't worry if you can't understand every word. Aim to get the general sense of the words, and the mood they suggest.

Use the task hints to help you plan. You could turn each hint into one branch of a quick Mind Map. Number the branches to put your ideas in order.

## HINTS ON THE SHAKESPEARE EXAM

Allow a few minutes at the end of the exam to check:

- Does your writing makes sense and flow from one idea to the next?
- Sentences: make sure you have used a full stop and capital for sentences where necessary – not just a comma.
- Quote-marks: use these where someone is speaking.
- Spelling, including the names of characters.

# GLOSSARY

**alliteration**   the repetition of words that begin with the same sound, e.g. *flashing fire will follow.*

**blank verse**   unrhymed verse composed in iambic pentameters (see below). In *Henry V* it is the speech of 'noble' characters.

**comic relief**   a light-hearted section or scene introduced into a serious play to lighten the mood.

**dramatic irony**   a situation where one or more characters on stage is unaware of some vital fact that the audience (and possibly other characters) know.

**iambic pentameter**   a line of verse with ten syllables and five beats or stresses. These are arranged in pairs, a weak syllable followed by a stressed one, to create a 'ti-tum, ti-tum' rhythm.

**imagery**   the use of 'word pictures' to make an idea come to life.

**malapropism**   using a word that sounds like the one intended but which has a different meaning to create little comic moments. Mistress Quickly uses malapropisms.

**metaphor**   a description of something as if it were something essentially different but also in some way similar; e.g. in Act 1, scene 2 Canterbury compares a well-run country to a beehive.

**personification**   describing something as if it were a person.

**pun**   playing on two different meanings of a word to create a joke.

**rhetorical questions**   a question which the speaker actually wants to give the answer to themselves. Often used in speeches to draw the audience in, not to make them call out the answer!

**rhyming couplet**   pair of lines which rhyme.

**soliloquy**   a speech in which a character speaks to the audience without any other characters hearing what is said.

Often they are speeches in which the character explains their thoughts and feelings or lay out plans.

**stage directions**  instructions to the actors, included in the text of the play.

**stereotypes**  Llewellyn, Jamy and Macmorris are stereotypes. They display characteristics that an audience might associate, often jokingly, with their nations, e.g. that all Scots are mean.

# INDEX

Agincourt 8, 43–61
'The army':
  Gower 9, 35–6, 40, 63
  Jamy 9, 35–6
  Llewellyn (Fluellen) 9,
    35–6, 40, 46, 58–60, 62–3
  MacMorris 9, 35–6

Bardolph 10, 29, 34
Bates 46, 48
Boy 10, 34–5, 56

Canterbury 10, 18–19
Charles IV (King of France)
  12, 30–1, 39
Chorus 14, 22–3, 43–4,
  61, 67
Church 16
Conspirators 9, 25–7, 72–4

Dauphin 12, 20, 30–1, 42,
  51, 67

Ely 10, 21
English nobles:
  Bedford 44
  Erpingham 8–9, 45
  Exeter 8–9, 19, 21, 26,
    31–2, 57
  Gloucester 8–9, 44
  Salisbury 8–9
  Suffolk 57
  Warwick 8–9
  Westmorland 8–9, 21, 26
  York 57

Falstaff 11, 25, 29

French nobles 12, 44, 50–1,
  57, 61, 64, 66

Governor of Harfleur 37

Harfleur 33–4, 35–7
Henry V 7–8, 16, 17–21, 23,
  25–7, 33, 37, 41, 44–8,
  52–61, 64–7
*Henry IV* (Parts 1 and 2)
  7, 11
Hostess (Mistress Quickly)
  10, 24, 63

Isabel (Queen of France) 12

Katherine 12, 38, 65–6

Mountjoy 41–2, 51, 59

Nym 10, 24, 29, 34

Patriotism 21, 23, 31, 35, 53
Pistol 10, 24, 29, 34, 40,
  45–6, 56, 62–3

Richard II 47

St Crispin's Day 52
Salic law 18
soliloquies 10, 34–5, 48,
  56, 63
soul 46–7
staging 14, 15, 52
style 15, 17, 21, 25, 28, 30,
  32, 34, 36, 39, 42, 49,
  53, 63, 66

Williams 8, 46–8, 59–61

# Buzan Training Courses

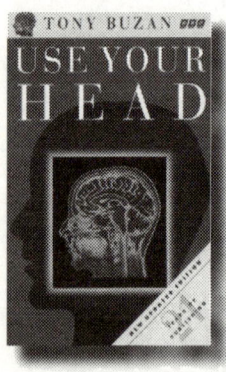

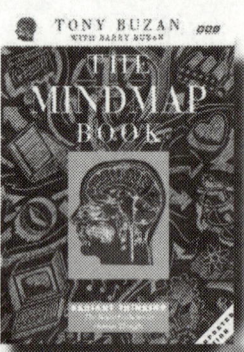

For further information on books, video and audio tapes, support materials and courses, please send for our brochure.

Buzan Centres Ltd, 54 Parkstone Road, Poole, Dorset, BH15 2PX
Tel: 44 (0) 1202 674676, Fax: 44 (0) 1202 674776
Email: Buzan_Centres_Ltd@compuserve.com